Praise for *When the Sisters Said Farewell*

"As a laywoman teaching in a Catholic school who walked through the experiences described in *When the Sisters Said Farewell*, I found Father Caruso's text insightful and reflective of the many ways transitions played out in schools and parishes when the sisters left. The interviews, which enrich the story, help the reader cherish the past and remain hopeful about the future. The history of this era in Catholic education must not be forgotten. This text will help us remember."—**Karen M. Ristau**, EdD, president, National Catholic Educational Association

"*When the Sisters Said Farewell* reads like a conversation around the convent's kitchen table, with the narrative sprinkled with experience as much as with data. Father Caruso captures the authentic pain of the American sisters' transition out the sacred space of their classrooms—and he does so with fairness, sowing a few seeds of hope along the way."—**Sister M. Paul McCaughey**, OP, superintendent, Office of Catholic Schools, Chicago, Illinois

"What is lost when Catholic schools close and disappear from American life? Father Michael Caruso, SJ, strikes an elegiac note in *When the Sisters Said Farewell*, a loving tribute to the crucial role women religious played in urban education. Sadly, like housework and laundry, the contributions of Catholic sisters become apparent only when they cease to exist."—**Ellen Skerrett**, author of *Born in Chicago: A History of Chicago's Jesuit University*

When the Sisters Said Farewell

The Transition of Leadership in Catholic Elementary Schools

Michael P. Caruso, SJ

ROWMAN & LITTLEFIELD EDUCATION

A division of
ROWMAN & LITTLEFIELD PUBLISHERS, INC.
Lanham • New York • Toronto • Plymouth, UK

Published by Rowman & Littlefield Education
A division of Rowman & Littlefield Publishers, Inc.
A wholly owned subsidiary of The Rowman & Littlefield Publishing Group, Inc.
4501 Forbes Boulevard, Suite 200, Lanham, Maryland 20706
http://www.rowmaneducation.com

10 Thornbury Road, Plymouth PL6 7PP, United Kingdom

British Library Cataloguing in Publication Information Available

Library of Congress Cataloging-in-Publication Data

Caruso, Michael P.
  When the sisters said farewell : the transition of leadership in Catholic elementary schools / Michael P. Caruso.
      p. cm.
  Includes bibliographical references and index.
  ISBN 978-1-61048-652-1 (cloth : alk. paper) — ISBN 978-1-61048-653-8 (pbk. : alk. paper) — ISBN 978-1-61048-654-5 (electronic)
  1. Catholic elementary schools—United States—History. 2. Nuns as teachers—United States—History. 3. Catholic Church—Education—United States—History. I. Title.
  LC501.C285 2012
  371.071'20973—dc23   2011047811

∞™ The paper used in this publication meets the minimum requirements of American National Standard for Information Sciences—Permanence of Paper for Printed Library Materials, ANSI/NISO Z39.48-1992.

Printed in the United States of America

I gratefully recognize everyone who believed in the value of this project and offered support and interest. I would like to dedicate this project to the students, colleagues, and families, past, present, and future, of Saint Ignatius College Prep in Chicago—*Ad Majorem Dei Gloriam*!

~

Contents

~

Foreword

Whenever the history of the Catholic Church in the United States is explored, an essential topic must be the contribution of women religious to the educational mission of the Church. From the early days of our nation, we saw the Ursuline sisters of colonial New Orleans educating the rich and poor. Our first bishop, John Carroll of Baltimore, was an indefatigable promoter of Catholic schools and a partner with Saint Elizabeth Ann Seton and the Sisters of Charity in launching the second-largest school system in the early days of the United States.

This network of parish and independent schools owes its life and vibrancy to the generosity of religious sisters. I never miss an opportunity to thank, praise, and recognize the excellent education imparted to me by the Sisters of Mercy at Holy Infant School in Ballwin, Missouri; my experience is not that different from legions of Catholics who were educated by these zealous teachers and administrators. They were not simply teachers, but also a part of our family and an integral part of the parish. The children they taught were the singular focus of their attention and lives; in loving and serving us, they were loving and serving their Lord. Our nation continues to reap this harvest that was planted by the teaching sisters. They taught us how to be active citizens and leaders for society and the Church.

That's why I'm so happy that Father Michael Caruso, SJ, has so wonderfully presented this important topic for the historical record. In a scholarly and very readable narrative, he captures a unique and compelling glimpse into a time of difficult transition of sisters withdrawing from schools. While their work has been, thank God, replicated by many able and competent laymen and laywomen, the presence and zeal of the sisters is an irreplaceable witness, unique to their vocation. I can tell you, as a shepherd of the Church, that these transitions have been difficult and traumatic for the sisters as well as the parish communities. But I can also tell you that there is promise and abundant hope for our schools in the men and women who lead them today. Much of that resilience is due to the lessons taught by the sisters.

If you attended a Catholic grammar school with sisters, I suspect this book will resonate with your experience. While you will be calling to mind your own parochial school days and the sisters who taught you, I hope you will also grow in appreciation for the sacrifices that were made for you. This book gives us a behind-the-scenes glimpse into the minds and hearts of those heroic women who built and sustained these schools. I am particularly pleased that the well-known statistics of diminishment of the teaching sisters are given flesh, bone, and voice in the experiences of those school leaders.

If you did not attend a Catholic grammar school or are not Catholic, I believe you will also find this book valuable. Father Caruso has set a context for this story of transition and graciously introduces the reader to his subject. Catholic schools remain an important force for good in our country. This book is a valuable tool to grasping a monumental time of transition. As a bishop and historian of the Church's story in the United States, I welcome this book and hope it will serve to inform and inspire, while stirring hearts of gratitude for an unparalleled contribution to education and the good of our nation.

+*Timothy M. Dolan*
Archbishop of New York
June 30, 2011

~

Acknowledgments

This book is the result of many years of study, research, and encouragement. The project was conceived when I was a professor of education at Loyola Marymount University in Los Angeles. The administration, along with my colleagues, gave tremendous support for telling this important story of Catholic schools. Dr. Mary McCullough was especially supportive as my mentor and dear friend; her insights and comments were always useful and supportive. The Jesuit Community at LMU, under the leadership of our rector, Father Robert Scholla, SJ, provided assistance in conducting the research as well as the fraternal encouragement to move the project to publication.

Many of my graduate students at Loyola Marymount were studying for degrees to serve as leaders in Catholic schools. They enjoyed studying the history of education to see how their own careers and vocations fit into the larger picture. The majority of these professionals were building upon the foundations set by the sisters you will read about in this book. Some of the questions addressed in this book are responses that developed from those stimulating discussions.

As a doctoral student at the University of San Francisco, I met visiting professor Dr. Thomas Hunt from the faculty at the University of Dayton and audited his course on the History of Catholic Schools. He was a great cheerleader for this project as well as a generous colleague who offered numerous suggestions to strengthen the text. Dr. Timothy Walch, who wrote the gold-standard *Parish School: American Catholic Parochial Education from Colonial Times to the Present*, was also a believer in this project. Mrs. Ann

xii   Acknowledgments

Carey, who has written extensively on many related topics, likewise offered insights regarding the style and substance of the narrative, so that the reader would have a better experience. My dissertation chair, Sister Mary Peter Traviss, OP, was also a great resource for approaching this topic and formulating good questions.

I would like to thank all of the sisters and laypeople who took part in the research. Some have chosen to remain anonymous and others are identified by their names. I thank Sister Elizabeth McGoldrick, SSL, the archivist of the Sisters of St. Louis in Woodland Hills, California; Sister Elizabeth was a tremendous ally in identifying key documents from her community. Sister Joanne Connolly, SSL, was a colleague at LMU and directed me to this congregation's legacy in southern California. Their heroic work is recounted in wonderful stories of the sacrifice and generosity of this community, which typifies so many other congregations. I discovered the correspondence between Mother Columbanus and then–Auxiliary Bishop Timothy Manning through the archives of the Sisters of St. Louis. However, I would also like to acknowledge the cooperation of the Archdiocese of Los Angeles and their permission to use those letters.

Sister Rita Smith, SCL, who was an art teacher of mine in high school, coordinated my visit and research with the Sisters of Charity of Leavenworth. It was a great blessing to reconnect with this community. The community archivist, Sister Kathleen M. Connelly, SCL, and her assistant, Sister Barbara Sellers, SCL, were very helpful in providing useful documents and photographs. I recall, during the visit to their motherhouse, going to the cemetery and seeing the graves of many former teachers and praying for their witness and vocations. Among the Sisters of Charity of Leavenworth who participated in the study, I wish to thank Sisters Mary Julitta Doerhoff, Regina Erbacher, Eileen Haynes, Ann McGuire, Mary Jane Schmitz, Elizabeth Skalicky, and Katherine Mary Weshues.

Sister Maureen Martin, ASCJ, was very helpful in connecting me with willing participants from her community of the Apostles of the Sacred Heart of Jesus. Sister Rita Amarante, ASCJ, who was my first-grade teacher, also provided helpful directions and transportation when visiting the motherhouse in Hamden, Connecticut. The community's archivist Sister Rita Petrarca, ASCJ, and her assistant, Kathy Larson, provided prompt and thorough assistance throughout the project. Among the Apostles of the Sacred Heart of Jesus who chose to be acknowledged, I heartily thank Sisters Susan Emmerich, Maureen Fitzgerald, Madeline Henry, Susan Marie Krupp, Eleanor Perfetto, Christian Price, Colleen Therese Smith, and John Martin Sullivan.

I had the pleasure of learning about a promising initiative by the Sisters of St. Joseph of Orange, California. Sister Judith Dugan, CSJ, who coordinates the program along with her assistant Sue LoPiccolo, offered useful insights into how communities of sisters can still offer support and leadership for schools.

Many laymen and laywomen gladly assisted with this project, but several chose to remain anonymous so that they could more freely express their views. The following educational leaders were happy to be acknowledged: Virginia "Ginny" Burns, Ann Halpin (RIP), Carol Lynn, Annabel McInerney, Ann Ortega, Paula Simpson, and Toni Walters.

Patrice Touhy and her patient staff from TrueQuest Communications, LLC, were angels from heaven; they prepared the manuscript for final submission to the editors, along with giving excellent advice about grammar, syntax, and readability.

~

Introduction

Ever-Present Teaching Sisters:
A Cherished Period

One of my earliest memories is of accompanying my mother, who was a frequent volunteer, to St. John the Baptist School in Kansas City, Missouri. There I was introduced not only to education but also to the wonderful sisters who taught there. Far from seeing them as exotic or aloof persons in their traditional habits, they were energetic and loving women with names and unique personalities. I recall the principal of that school, the Mother Superior, selling squirt guns to students at the annual school picnic, something that would have been unthinkable in many other schools, and perhaps scandalous to other orders of sisters.

It was inconceivable to think of a Catholic elementary school without sisters, yet history has proven the implausible possible. There was a time in the not-so-distant past when almost every parish consisted of four buildings: the church, the rectory that housed the priests, the school, and the convent that housed the sisters. Over the years those convents emptied and became offices or were used for other purposes. Sisters seemed to disappear almost imperceptibly.

Many have wondered what became of the teaching sisters and why those convents are often no longer occupied as residences. The sisters reached out not only to Catholics but to all people of goodwill; for many Americans, they were the face of Catholicism in the United States. The reduced number of sisters in education ministry and the fewer number of sisters overall is a concern shared by all levels of the Church. That concern is certainly related to the great debt of gratitude U.S. Catholics have for women religious who served as educators during a pivotal period of growth and prosperity in American history.

After World War II (1945) and through the years that followed the Second Vatican Council (1962–1965), the Catholic Church in the United States experienced tremendous growth, followed by a steep decline. This boom and bust phenomenon was best illustrated in the enormous expansion of Catholic elementary schools and its corollary of growth in the communities of religious sisters who largely provided the workforce for these schools as principals and teachers. There was a time in which no one could have dreamed of Catholic schools without sisters teaching in them. However, from coast to coast, there was a rapid and dramatic departure of sisters from those schools. While active Catholics might be aware of the general facts of this transition, few people have heard the story in extensive detail. The sisters tell this story in their own words.

What was the exit experience like for those sisters who were the last members of their community to serve in a Catholic elementary school as teachers or administrators? What happened after the sisters left those schools, and who were the people who took their places? What challenges did the people who followed the sisters face? What is the educational legacy of these sisters? This book will address those questions by presenting the voices of some of the remarkable and generous people who contributed to the growth and vigor of the Catholic school system in uncertain times.

In the pages that follow, the school stories of many sisters reveal a pivotal moment in the history of each parish. Sometimes when sisters left the parish school, the departure unfolded out of the view of many parishioners and school families. In other instances their withdrawal was dramatic and painful. This is the story of when Catholic religious sisters said farewell to educational ministry in various elementary schools across the United States and about the laymen and laywomen who stepped into these leadership roles. It is a story about the expansive school system that was built and has shrunk since the mid-1960s. It is also a story of the legacy of an education the sisters gave to generations of Catholics.

It is an unfinished story whose destiny now primarily lies in the hands of generous laypeople who wish to build upon the foundation laid by the sisters. The religious sisters and laypeople who forged this historical transition have unique stories to tell. Many participants expressed intense feelings of sadness or anger in sharing their stories, especially when the recollections stirred up unresolved disagreements with decisions made by leaders that they had to implement. Some distrusted the processes for reaching decisions to withdraw from a school. Sometimes authorities lacked accurate information and, in some cases, did not follow the specified process.

As Catholic education enters its third millennium, it continues to face the chronic struggle to find adequate financial resources. Too often the burden of maintaining a high-quality school and paying just wages and benefits outpaces the discretionary funds of families. As the narrative explores the monumental contribution and transition Catholic teaching sisters faced in the past century, it also presents a challenge to a new generation of leaders to continue the educational legacy of the sisters.

The experience of teaching sisters and pioneering laypeople continue to provide instructive lessons. They serve as wisdom figures and their fascinating stories are worth gathering and giving attention to. This book takes a close look at a time when the religious sisters could no longer sustain their wildly generous gift of an affordable parochial school system throughout the United States.

Chapter 1, "What Led to the Massive Catholic School System?," begins by introducing the reader to the historical themes that run throughout the chronicle of Catholic schools. The nineteenth-century United States was suspicious and hostile toward Catholic immigrants; this animosity became embedded in textbooks and lessons and played out in schools. Under the leadership of courageous leaders like Archbishop John Hughes of New York, attempts were made to secure funding for parochial schools. The financing of Catholic schools became an obstacle as state governments began enacting laws specifically denying funds to any religious school.

Building an extensive Catholic school system would take a huge labor force that would work for mere subsistence; women religious accepted this challenge and filled the roles of principals and teachers. As a benefit to the sisters, their schools became the places where young women, attracted to their way of life and work, could go. Two characteristics emerged from the ministry of these teaching sisters: they responded to the injustices of religious bigotry, and they provided a financial subsidy in human resources for the teaching project. These two characteristics became the hallmarks of sister educators.

As the Catholic population grew from waves of immigration during the nineteenth and early twentieth centuries, a visionary plan was declared by the Third Council of Baltimore. The bishops of the United States foresaw a Catholic elementary school in every parish across the country. Financing and building the schools was one issue, but finding the teaching sisters would be another.

Chapter 2, "Finding the Sisters," illustrates how the burgeoning post–World War II Archdiocese of Los Angeles secured the services of the Sisters of St. Louis from Ireland. The correspondence presents the urgent needs of both the sisters and the schools. Practical issues that the communities of sisters had to face upon their arrival are brought into focus. While each community of sisters would have a unique story to tell about their educational ministries, the story of the Sisters of St. Louis offers a paradigm of generosity and courage in responding to the needs of the growing church. It is an instructive model of many sisters who responded to the call to teach.

Chapter 3, "Preparing the Sisters for Teaching, Making Sacrifices," describes how sisters were prepared to teach in elementary schools. The mentoring system was the dominant model of teacher preparation supplemented by academic degrees and official credentials.

This chapter also looks at the great sacrifices sisters made. By offering their services in return for a minimal stipend, the sisters lived a frugal lifestyle with little security.

Chapter 4, "From the Motherhouse to the Classroom," illustrates the culture that imbued Catholic elementary schools, which was chiefly carried from the motherhouse of religious communities. A pervasive Catholic identity animated these schools. The reader is introduced to two religious communities who participated in the project: the Apostles of the Sacred Heart of Jesus and the Sisters of Charity of Leavenworth. Through interviews, the sisters describe their schools and what they felt was unique in their community's educational philosophy.

In chapter 5, "Working with Pastors," the relationship of pastors with the schools and the sisters is explored. These relationships were and continue to be pivotal for the success or demise of a school. This chapter also looks at how lay teachers partnered with sisters in staffing Catholic schools.

Chapter 6, "Changes in Religious Life Lead to Departures," presents the confluence of events within society and religious life that led to sisters withdrawing from schools. The renewal of religious life as directed by Vatican II would be interpreted in a variety of ways; some of these directions had a catastrophic impact on Catholic schools, especially when sisters were allowed to find their own ministry. A hypothetical school is presented, which tells a plausible story of the diminishment of sisters working at the school in the open-placement system. This chapter continues the story of sisters moving into apostolates where they would have more direct contact with the poor; this often meant not being in Catholic elementary schools.

Chapter 7, "The Sisters Reflect upon Their Experiences," offers reflections of sisters who were the last members of their communities to serve in

Catholic elementary schools. There are descriptions of how this sad news was announced and how the unwelcome news was received and the criteria for making the decision to withdraw.

Chapter 8, "When a School Closed," recounts school closures and the relationship of diminishing numbers of sisters. It looks at what happened to schools owned by the community and also summarizes the impact of the open-placement system on Catholic schools.

Chapter 9, "Lay Leadership Emerges," introduces the laymen and laywomen who stepped forward to continue the Catholic school project. Many of these leaders pioneered new working relationships and expectations with the pastors, which were often painful and difficult. Paying living salaries to the laity and not having the workforce living on the parish campus presented a learning curve. As the importance of Vatican II's emphasis on the baptismal gifts was being embraced, the parish leadership was challenged with new demands and realities.

Chapter 10, "Transition and Signs of Renewal," describes how the educational legacy of the sisters has continued as young laymen and laywomen step forth to staff schools. The University of Notre Dame's Alliance for Catholic Education program—and related programs—are presented as an important response to the historic challenge of funding schools with a workforce of novice teachers. This chapter also presents advice about leadership change flowing from the reflections of women religious who became experts in facing change.

Chapter 11, "The Future of Catholic Schools and the Legacy of the Sisters," looks to the future of Catholic elementary schools and the ways that religious communities might still contribute. The Educational Network of the Sisters of St. Joseph of Orange, California, is discussed. The leadership degree programs offered by Catholic higher education are outlined along with the necessary knowledge and competencies for school leaders. This chapter ends with a summary of steps that can help ensure a bright future for Catholic schools.

CHAPTER ONE

~

What Led to the Massive Catholic School System?

The image of the Catholic elementary school has earned a permanent place in the cultural imagination of the United States. Films, plays, cartoons, television shows, comedians, writers, and dramatists have all tried to capture the experience of a Catholic school education.

Sometimes the portrayals are serious and affecting, as in John Patrick Shanley's 2005 Pulitzer Prize– and Tony Award–winning play *Doubt*, which explored the reactions of two Sisters of Charity to an allegation of sexual abuse made against the assistant pastor. There are also lighthearted works, such John R. Powers's popular book and musical *Do Black Patent Leather Shoes Really Reflect Up?* or the theatrical spoof *Late Nite Catechism*. But often the image of Catholic schools is stereotyped as a spiritual boot camp strictly administered by martinet women religious mistakenly, though tenaciously, called nuns. (Canonically, a "nun" belongs to a cloistered or contemplative order and a "sister" is part of an apostolic or active religious community.)

It is highly probable that if people were asked about their first association with the term "Catholic school," the picture of a religious sister dressed in a traditional habit would be the most likely response, even though many people have not seen such attire in half a century. (As part of the renewal of Vatican II, men's communities modified the practice of wearing the habit; the majority of women's communities initially modified their habits and then many eventually chose to wear secular clothing with an identifiable symbol such as a community pin or cross.)

People today, even active Catholics, are somewhat amazed to learn that many Catholic schools do not have any sisters working in them. This is not to say that all Catholic elementary schools are without sisters, but this number has diminished significantly in the past forty-five years (see table 1.1 and figure 1.1). So what accounts for this persistence of memory? Why do people associate Catholic schools with women religious even when the reality of their presence in these schools has diminished so dramatically?

Perhaps this persistence of memory correlates to the outstanding education provided to generations of Catholics at a time of national growth in the first three-quarters of the twentieth century. These years—inclusive of two world wars; the rise of fascism, socialism, and communism; and a global depression—correlated with a growing Catholic population that filled the urban landscape with parishes reflecting a diversity of European ethnic identities. Because the public schools in the United States were basically Protestant and anti-Catholic, these parishes typically had schools of their own, and in many instances the parishes began their building campaigns by

Table 1.1. Post–Vatican II Decline of Teaching Sisters and Catholic Elementary Schools

Year	Teaching Sisters	Catholic Elementary Schools
1965	104,314	113,446
1980	41,135	9,676
2002	8,233	8,292
2009	5,169	5,772
2011	4,977	5,848

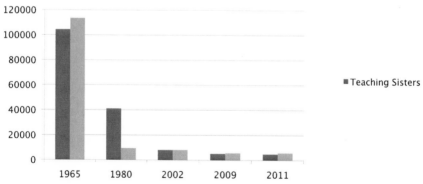

Figure 1.1. Post–Vatican II Decline of Teaching Sisters and Catholic Elementary Schools

Note: "Teaching Sisters" represents sisters teaching in elementary and secondary schools, as well as CCD programs and higher education. The number of sisters teaching specifically in elementary schools has not been disaggregated. Nonetheless, this correlation is instructive.

first establishing the school building with the hope of one day moving the worshipping community out of the gymnasium into a legitimate church. Many a parish never realized that dream. This sequence follows the tradition and wisdom of New York archbishop John Hughes, who wrote in a pastoral letter, "Schoolhouse first and churches afterward."[1]

Education and Anti-Catholicism

The dynamics, challenges, and aspirations of the Golden Age of Catholic schools during most of the last century are tied to the themes of Catholic migration to the United States and many of the forgotten lessons of that era, which remain instructive for today. In *Parish School: American Catholic Parochial Education from Colonial Times to the Present* (2003), Timothy Walch identifies five enduring historical characteristics of Catholic elementary schools in the United States: community, immigration, survival, adaptability, and identity.

The contributions and legacy of the religious sisters embrace each of these marks: the sisters were on the forefront of the Catholic community; many were the daughters of immigrants or were generous missionaries who emigrated to the United States to help their people; the sacrifices that women religious made substantiated the survival of the schools; the sisters were creative in adapting schools to the times; and the presence of sisters in a school confirmed its strong Catholic identity.

The momentum for establishing urban Catholic schools was primarily fueled by the religiously hostile environment encountered by the waves of Catholic immigrants coming to America's shores—nearly eight million during the nineteenth century.[2] Jay P. Dolan in *The American Catholic Experiment* described the Irish portion of this immigration figure:

> Long before the potato blight, people had been leaving Ireland in rather impressive numbers; in fact, between 1820 and 1840, more than 260,000 Irish emigrated to America. Once the famine struck, however, the exodus escalated dramatically, and in a brief, six-year period, 1846–51, over one million people left Ireland. The passing of the famine hardly halted the flow of migration, with the result that, between 1851 and 1920, 3.3 million Irish immigrants settled in the United States, bringing the total Irish migration to the United States, during this hundred-year period, 1820–1920, to 4.3 million people.[3]

This tsunami of immigrants posed serious challenges and threats to the existing urban population. In *The Great School Wars: New York City, 1805–*

1973, Diane Ravitch lucidly illustrated the paradigm that is replicated through the history of the nation by looking at New York City in the 1790s:

> Though the town of New York had not yet experienced any large-scale immigration, native New Yorkers already associated immigration with crime and poverty. There was a reality to their attitude, since newcomers were more likely to be poor than the native-born, and most criminals were reported to be foreigners. There is no more constant theme in the unfolding of New York City's history than the reciprocal relationship between the native and the immigrant: the immigrant arrives poor, lives in crowded slums with others like himself, suffers discrimination and terrible living conditions, and (as a group) produces a disproportionate number of criminals and paupers; the native blames the immigrant for bringing crime, poverty, and slums to the city, discriminates against him, and wonders whether *this* particular group can ever be assimilated into American society. With each major wave of immigration— Irish, Italians, Jews, blacks, Puerto-Ricans—the scenario has been replayed. And in each instance, the cultural clash of the old and the new has occurred in and around the school.[4] (emphasis in original)

No film has dealt better with these immigrant-native tensions than Martin Scorsese's *Gangs of New York* (2002). The Nativist movement and the American Native Party sought to harass and discriminate against Irish Catholics. The deep attitudes of antipathy toward Catholics were tied to the misguided understanding that the authority of the pope would extend beyond spiritual realms and intrude into the direct governance of the United States should there ever be a Catholic majority. Since Catholics were typically portrayed as being hostile to American ideals of democracy, it was presumed that being a practicing Catholic was irreconcilable with being a good American citizen.

There were attempts to minimize opportunities for Catholics. This stance even applied to employment and the right to hold public office. These sentiments were promoted by Nativist Party leaders, such as inventor Samuel F. B. Morse, in popular leaflets of the day. Further, these anti-Catholic attitudes, synonymous with anti-immigration agendas, were institutionalized within the ranks of the Know-Nothing Party, which grew in the 1850s, and were also often mirrored in the policies and platforms of the Republican Party.

In Philadelphia, the Bible Riots of the 1840s arose from the compulsory reading of the King James Version of the Bible in public schools, a version that was repugnant to immigrant Catholics who fled religious persecution at the hands of oppressive British policies. When Archbishop Francis Kenrick (1796–1863) appealed to the authorities to use the Catholic-approved Douai-Rhiems version for the Roman Catholic students and that students be excused from Protestant catechetical classes, tensions ignited.

Churches were burned and the militia was called to restore order. The common schools of this period were undisputedly Protestant schools and financed with public funds.[5] Textbooks and lessons were full of contemptuous illustrations and examples that derided Catholicism and subjected its young adherents to lessons that undermined the faith of their families.

Archbishop John Hughes (1797–1864), known as Dagger John,[6] like Kenrick in Philadelphia, was an immigrant from Ireland and fought these same battles in New York but with a different strategy. As John J. Hennesey recounts in *American Catholics* (1983), when rumors reached Hughes that Catholic properties were at risk of arson, as in Philadelphia, he warned the Nativist mayor, "Should one Catholic come to harm, or should one Catholic church or business be molested, we shall turn his city into a second Moscow."[7]

Hughes's allusion to Moscow stemmed from the generally known fact that the citizens of Moscow preferred self-destruction to allowing Napoleon access and use of the city; this reference was not lost on the New York establishment, which knew Hughes to be a man of his word and a force to be reckoned with. Civil unrest was avoided, and Hughes would turn his attention to Catholic schools and education as a means of advancing the plight of the poor.

Parish schools were being established in several large cities such as Philadelphia, Baltimore, and New York. Hughes made a case for distributing taxes for education according to the school chosen by the taxpayer, so the money would follow the child and benefit the school. Hughes entered into public debates to plead this cause, but the measure ultimately failed. Yet the public discourse helped curtail the most egregious and bigoted Catholic references found in the schools and particularly in textbooks. The strategies for neutralizing religious differences would eventually lead to secularizing public schools. This process of secularization remains an area of public debate to this day.

Hennesey notes that the prejudice encountered by the Irish in the United States would be replicated for each immigrant group: "By the time massive Italian immigration began around 1880, the American church and American Catholics were already rather set in their ways, and those ways were too often not the ways of the new arrivals."[8]

This hostility and rejection, says Hennesey, came "not only from old Americans, but from . . . their coreligionists."[9] Dolan also notes this same phenomenon in describing the establishment of parishes: "Even though they might have lived in the same area of the city, German and Irish Cath-olics were not willing to worship in the same church. Each group wanted to worship and pray in its own language, following the tradition and customs of the Old World."[10]

In large cities of the East and Midwest, parishes and schools with different languages and nationalities were established across the street or down the block from one another at a time when there was one unifying and official language of worship. St. Bridget's (Irish), St. Mary's (German), St. Stanislaus (Polish), and Our Lady of the Holy Rosary (Italian) might have been four parishes all within a few blocks of one another.

Baltimore's James Cardinal Gibbons (1834–1921) had been an advocate of unifying these groups. "He urged that Catholics respect each other's heritages and form a United States–minded church on other than cumber-some and contentious national lines."[11] In *Catholic School Leadership: An Invitation to Lead*, the editors summarized the building of schools in the late nineteenth and early twentieth centuries when they noted, "Much of the drive for Catholic schools emanated from the desire to preserve ethnic heritage."[12]

An established ethnic group would complain about the strange language, dress, smells of food, bad hygiene, and lack of manners and trustworthiness of the new group. As Suellen Hoy describes it in *Good Hearts: Catholic Sisters in Chicago's Past*, "St. Joseph's was a part, but a separate part, of the large Jesuit parish of Holy Family, then made up mostly of Italians [1933]. In the 1890s, the Irish and German parishioners who had built the impressive Gothic church on Roosevelt Road had not welcomed the Italians, and the Italians in turn refused to accept black migrants in the 1930s."[13]

If there has been any group of people in the history of the United States who should have known through hard lessons of persecution how to treat the newcomer, it should have been Roman Catholics, but that was not always the case. Perhaps if they were better organized or had a stronger sense of what united them, the prejudices might have been faced more systematically, but instead local squabbles carried the day.

Improbable Reversals: Politics and School Funding

While Catholics themselves were in conflict, together they continued to face opposition from the Protestant majority. In *American Catholicism* (1969), John Tracy Ellis notes that as the Catholic population grew and such anti-Catholic prejudice could not be as overt, the bigotry was usu-ally made manifest in campaigns against using public funds for sectarian schools—that is, Catholic schools. Republican Representative James G. Blaine from Maine would propose an amendment in 1875 to the United States Constitution banning any public funding for religious schools, but it failed to pass. Nonetheless, the enthusiasm for this "Blaine Amendment" would spread to thirty-eight states and find a way into the state constitutions since education is specifically a financial responsibility of the state. The Tenth Amendment of the United States Constitution gives to the states the responsibility of education, since it is not covered in the Constitution ("The powers not delegated to the United States by the Constitution, nor prohibited by it to the States, are reserved to the States respectively, or to the people").

President Ulysses S. Grant made the following remarks in Des Moines, Iowa, in 1876, which would further fuel a bias against funding of religious schools and, of course, was a clear signal to his audience of not assisting Catholic schools:

> Encourage free schools and resolve that not one dollar of the money appropriated to their support shall be appropriated to the support of any sectarian school; that neither the state or nation, not both combined, shall support institutions of learning other than those sufficient to afford to every child in the land the opportunity of a good common-school education, unmixed with sectarian, pagan, or atheistical dogma.[14]

The Blaine Amendments were seemingly insurmountable and imbued with a nascent anti-Catholic purpose.

> Though not always mentioned, Catholic schools were the target for the proposals of Grant and Blaine. Both Grant and Blaine were among a growing number of Americans who were vocal about their anti-Catholic positions. Furthermore, the congressional record on the Blaine Amendment debates reveals (1) the underlying anti-Catholic sentiment among amendment advocates and (2) the focus of the amendment on Catholic schools.[15]

Almost a decade later (in 1884) James G. Blaine would build upon this Catholic prejudice as he championed the Republican aversion to rum (the temperance movement), Romanism (the xenophobic geist aimed at Catholic immigrants), and rebellion (a reference to the Civil War) in his failed campaign for the presidency against the Democratic nominee and winner, Grover Cleveland. Blaine wanted to exploit the anti-Catholic feelings of the time, but he was roundly defeated as Catholic immigrants continued to flood into the country.

It is cause for concern and reflection how legislation—namely, the Blaine Amendments that are part of most state constitutions, which were formulated out of anti-Catholic bigotry—has gained respectability and the automatic allegiance of much of the educational establishment, especially of influential teachers' unions.

Perhaps the most bizarre paradox in this chapter of nineteenth-century American educational history is that James Blaine was baptized as a Catholic and most likely received some Catholic religious instruction. Among his Catholic relatives were Ellen Ewing Sherman, wife of General William T. Sherman, and Mother Angela Gillespie, CSC, the foundress of the Sisters of the Holy Cross in the United States, which established several dozen Catholic schools across the country.[16]

This brief review of some of the nineteenth-century immigrant Catholic experience is a preface to understanding the leadership of women religious in the twentieth century. One of the most enduring challenges and predictable dynamics in American culture is its xenophobia. New immigrant groups to the United States are subjected to the same suspicions, questions, and criticisms that Catholic immigrants experienced in the nineteenth century.

The Catholic Church built the largest private school system in the world to serve these immigrants, and congregations of sisters provided the workforce to help these people find their way in their new homeland. Their commitment to staffing these schools subsidized a system that was denied financial assistance through public funding.

The bishops of the United States, concerned about the diminution of the faith and the importance of getting an education to move forward in society, addressed the importance of parochial schools at the Third Plenary Council of Baltimore in 1884. Among their mandates was the establishment of a Catholic school in every parish where it was feasible.

If a parish established a school as directed by the Council of Baltimore, pastors admonished parents to place their children in these schools; sometimes the admonition was a threat of committing mortal sin if a parent did not comply. Parishioners may have built a school while making great sacrifices.

The religious communities were also convinced that this was a noble dream and were committed to providing the workforce. As the Church entered the twentieth century, the schools were staffed almost entirely by women religious from various communities. While the number of schools was increasing, so was the establishment of motherhouses where congregations would provide formation for their new sister recruits. The next chapter will describe the monumental task of finding the workforce of sisters and preparing them as educators.

CHAPTER TWO

~

Finding the Sisters

During the post–World War II years, the United States experienced a phenomenal growth spurt producing the Baby Boom generation (1946–1964); seventy-five million children were born during this era.[1] Throughout this same time period, in vast numbers never before seen nor likely to be seen again, women entered religious life. While some joined the growing Catholic network of hospitals and health care, the majority were assigned to teach in the rising number of Catholic schools.

Given the history of Catholics in the United States, it should come as no surprise that sisters typically came from large families with strong ethnic ties. Indeed it was not untypical in places like St. Louis, Missouri, to have motherhouses of large congregations identified with an ethnicity, which may have influenced a woman's choice of community. If a young woman grew up in a predominantly Irish or German parish and had been educated by a congregation of that ethnic tradition, she would know this group best and be inclined to enter that community. The communities also sent young women from their European motherhouses to the United States. As Dolan notes in *The American Catholic Experiment*, "Numerous religious orders were transplanted to the United States from various parts of Europe, and they, too, became involved in teaching: 91 of the 119 women's religious communities in the nineteenth century were European or Canadian in origin."[2]

Catholics in Post–World War II Los Angeles

Consider the growth in the Archdiocese of Los Angeles, California, during the episcopacy of James Francis Cardinal McIntyre (1947–1970). In *His Eminence of Los Angeles: James Francis Cardinal McIntyre*, Msgr. Francis J. Weber notes that upon his arrival in Los Angeles, Cardinal McIntyre conducted a survey about the needs of the archdiocese. He discovered that while Catholic high schools enrolled 10,246 students, there were 41,754 students who wanted to be in Catholic high schools, but the schools had not been established in areas of growth.[3] Similarly, Catholic elementary schools enrolled 48,608 students with another 52,392 unable to enroll due to a lack of schools or space in the schools. The Youth Education Fund was launched to address the needs of the archdiocesan school system, which at the time was the second-largest provider of educational services in California.

To care for the influx of one thousand Catholics weekly, the Archdiocese of Los Angeles from 1948 to 1963 had been establishing a new parish every sixty-six days and building a new school every twenty-six days.[4] Though the rapid growth of Los Angeles is unparalleled in the United States, it does reflect the unprecedented growth that took place throughout the country in this post–World War II period to greater and lesser degrees.

Cardinal McIntyre was a controversial leader during and after his tenure as archbishop in Los Angeles, but no one can doubt his determination and love for Catholic schools, which he made evident in his aggressive building campaign.[5] In 1953 the University of Notre Dame cited him as "America's Cardinal of Education." During Cardinal McIntyre's episcopacy he dedicated approximately 179 educational facilities, which were primarily new schools, school renovations, school expansions, gymnasiums, convents, or other education-related facilities.

These schools needed teachers, legions of teachers, and they needed them quickly. The Daughters of Charity were the first sisters to arrive in Los Angeles in 1856, when they opened a school and orphanage. Many other orders of religious sisters would follow and establish schools and provincial houses in the area.

The Sisters of St. Louis and the Schools of Los Angeles

During this postwar period of expansion in the 1940s and 1950s, it was presumed that sisters would continue to staff the expanding Catholic school system. But communities such as the Sisters of St. Joseph of Carondelet and of Orange, the Sisters of Mercy, the Dominican Sisters of Mission San José, and many others were already stretched to their limits. Cardinal McIntyre needed to extend the search for teaching sisters beyond the borders of California and the United States. Through his chancellor, Bishop Timothy Manning, a very generous group of sisters was found in the Irish Province of the Sisters of St. Louis. Perhaps in their story one can find varying echoes and reflections of every other group of women religious who responded to the great educational project in the United States at that time. In describing their mission, the sisters write on their website (www.stlouissisters.org),

> Our founder, Louis Marie Eugene Bautain, was guided by the Spirit of *Sint Unum*—May they be one. His passion of one world, healed, unified, and transformed, continues to inspire all we do today. Our patron is St. Louis IX, whose feast day is August 25th. The Institute was approved by Rome in July, 1844. It spread to Ireland in 1859, where two years later the group had to separate from France on demand of the Irish bishop. It continued to spread around the world—to England in 1912, to Ghana in 1947, Nigeria in 1948, and the United States in 1949. In 1952 the French group amalgamated with the motherhouse in Ireland. After the call of Vatican II to send religious to Latin America, it spread to Brazil in 1977.

While it might be expedient to say that Bishop Manning contacted the Sisters of St. Louis and they sent the first of many contingents, too much history would be lost in not reading the actual correspondence between His Excellency and Mother Mary Columbanus, the Superior General at the time.[6] The letters illustrate the great urgency of the educational project, and the real concerns of the sisters who would travel halfway around the world from Monaghan, Ireland, to Los Angeles to start a new foundation.

Letter 1

ARCHDIOCESE OF LOS ANGELES
714 WEST OLYMPIC BOULEVARD
LOS ANGELES 15 CALIFORNIA
December 3, 1948

Sister Superior
Lake Monaghan
County Monaghan
Ireland

My Dear Sister Superior:

Here in Los Angeles there has been a phenomenal growth in population in the last few years. Our Catholic population has increased in proportion.

The Most Reverend Archbishop, and his priests, are much concerned about providing a Catholic education for the children. Already there are over 60,000 provided for in our Catholic Schools. We are undertaking a program of school construction that will partially satisfy the need. Our most pressing difficulty is supplying the teaching Sisters for these schools. It is an apostolic labor that is productive of a great harvesting, and carries with it the abundant blessings of Almighty God.

We have in the Archdiocese over forty-five different communities of Sisters, and thanks be to God, there is an increase in the number of vocations to the sisterhood each year.

This letter is written to inquire if your Community would be interested, and in a position to assume the responsibility for teaching in one or more of these new schools. The average school handles about 450 children, with one Sister being assigned to each of the eight grades. In most cases a modern convent is provided for the Sisters.

I would be very happy if I might have a word from you in reply to this inquiry. I know that our Most Reverend Archbishop would be happy to provide the traveling expenses of any Sisters that would come under these circumstances.

Praying every blessing upon you, I am
Very sincerely yours,

+Timothy Manning
Auxiliary Bishop of Los Angeles
Chancellor

Letter 2

Convent of St. Louis,
MONAGHAN.
12th December 1948

My Lord,

I thank His Excellency the Archbishop and you for the gracious invitation to work in the Archdiocese of Los Angeles. On this grey, cold, rainy December day the sunny skies of California make a certain appeal, though perhaps you are just now longing for a "soft day" and a wisp of Irish mist. Your letter came on the Vigil of the Feast of the Immaculate Conception which gives it a special significance. I have discussed the matter with the Mothers of the Council, and before coming to a decision we would like some information on the following points:

1. What Academic qualifications are needed in your Primary Schools? Our Primary School Sisters are either:

   (a) trained in Ireland.
   (b) trained in England or Scotland.

(c) *Certificated or recognized as Salaried Assistants in Ireland or England. Among these latter are some who have special qualifications in Music, Elocution, Hand-crafts, or who hold the Montessori Diploma. Many of these are better teachers and would be more useful generally than some College trained Sisters.*

2. *Would a Staff of eight Sisters be needed to start with? We could not give eight out of any one of the above categories, probably some out of each group would be selected for reasons of general suitability. A copy of the Education Scheme, Syllabus, etc. would be helpful.*
3. *In what place exactly do you propose to open the School and to what Nationality would the pupils belong?*
4. *Would you build and equip Convent and Schools?*
5. *What income would the Sisters have and what type of contract would be made with the Congregation? If there is a recognised form I should be glad to get a specimen copy.*

I very gratefully appreciate the offer to pay the Sisters' travelling expenses, as to be quite candid, we are not in a position to undertake any financial responsibility. Our Sisters would I feel sure give generous, efficient co-operation in the Apostolic work of your great Archdiocese.

May I ask your holy prayers that we may do God's Will in this matter. Wishing you all the blessings of the Holy Season.

I am, My Lord,
Yours sincerely in J.C.,

Mother Colombanus
Superior General

Letter 3

ARCHDIOCESE OF LOS ANGELES
714 WEST OLYMPIC BOULEVARD
LOS ANGELES 15 CALIFORNIA
December Eighteenth 1948

Mother M. Columbanus, Superior General
CONENT [sic] OF ST. LOUIS
Monaghan
County Monaghan, Ireland.

My dear Mother Comuanus [sic]:

This will acknowledge your esteemed letter of December 12th. By strange coincidence, we also had "soft weather" when your letter arrived, which is unusual for us in California.

I am enclosing herewith a manual for teachers in our elementary schools, and also a sample form which may answer most of the questions you have in mind. There [are] no compulsory requirements of State Law in California for academic qualifications. However, in our Catholic colleges during the summer sessions and also on Saturdays, courses are provided for the Degree of Bachelor of Arts, after which State credentials may be obtained.

A staff of eight Sisters would not be essential to start off with, but a Sister qualified in music and hand-crafts would be very welcome.

The schools that require teaching Sisters are all located in the vicinity of Los Angeles. The schools are not exclusive for any one nationality, though in some instances the predominant attendance would be Mexican.

The present salary for each Sister is $50.00 per month, for twelve months.

We respectfully hope and pray that you will find it possible to accept our offer. There is one new school in particular that we have in mind. A modern type of building, with very new and modern convent, is already constructed.

With sentiments of esteem, I am
Very sincerely yours,

+Timothy Manning
Auxiliary Bishop of Los Angeles
Chancellor

Letter 4

Convent of St. Louis
Monaghan.
20th January 1949

My Lord,

I must apologize for my delay in replying to your very helpful letter but I was called away to attend the obsequies of a Sister who died rather suddenly in a branch House. We have decided to accept the Foundation provided we can spare the Sisters. How many would be needed to start and when? The Superior would probably be in charge of the School and a Sister would look after the housekeeping and give some help in the School. I expect there would be a maid to help with housework. My question about the nationality of the pupils did not I hope give you the impression that we have any objection to a mixture of races. It is entirely from the apostolic angle that we have considered the question and please God we shall have plenty of opportunities of working for souls. May I beg your holy prayers that we may do God's Will in all that concerns this affair. With every kind wish,

I am, My Lord,
Yours sincerely in J.C.

M. Columbanus

Letter 5

ARCHDIOCESE OF LOS ANGELES
714 WEST OLYMPIC BOULEVARD
LOS ANGELES 15 CALIFORNIA
January Twenty-seventh 1949

Reverend Mother N. Columbanus
CONVENT OF ST. LOUIS
Lakeview Monaghan
County Monaghan
Ireland

My dear Mother Columbanus:

Your letter of January 20th has brought us much joy in knowing that you would be able to come to Los Angeles to staff a school.

The particular school the Most Reverend Archbishop has in mind at this time is the school of the Nativity Parish, in El Monte, which is a suburb of Los Angeles. The Convent and School are both newly constructed buildings, with all modern conveniences.

The school has been in operation for a year already, with another community temporarily in charge, so that the problem of starting a new school is diminished considerably.

We would like to have eight or nine Sisters to staff the school. It will be essential for us to have immediately the names of the Sisters who will be coming, so that we may issue the letters for them to the American Consul. There is a considerable time consumed in obtaining immigration visas, and we should not delay, so that everything will be ready by September.

With every blessing, I am
Very sincerely yours,

+Timothy Manning
Auxiliary Bishop of Los Angeles
Chancellor

Letter 6

Convent of St. Louis
Monaghan
8th February 1949

My Lord,

In answer to your kind letter I am going to try your patience by asking some further questions,

1. *Could we begin with six Sisters? I fear we could not give eight for September.*
2. *Will you kindly confirm that travel expenses will be defrayed by His Grace the Archbishop?*
3. *Who will pay the traveling expenses of delegates to the General Chapter in the Mother House and of Sisters for a holiday there every six years?*
4. *Does Article X in the Agreement with the Pastor prevent the Sisters receiving gifts "intuitu personae"?*
5. *What hope is there of attaining financial security for further development over and above the maintenance allowance from the Pastor? Can we look forward to establishing our own High Schools later on? These could be a fruitful source of Vocations to the Congregation—apart from their usefulness to the church and state.*

I wish there were no need to put such mercenary questions but as I have explained in a former letter the Congregation is already burdened with debts for buildings, etc. In giving eight Sisters we are forfeiting Salaries of at least £2000 per year—not to mention the amount spent in their training. Each new foundation is expected, in time, to make some return to the Mother House.

Asking your blessing and with every good wish.

I am, my Lord,
Yours sincerely in J.C.

Mother Columbanus
SUPERIOR GENERAL.

Letter 7

ARCHDIOCESE OF LOS ANGELES
714 WEST OLYMPIC BOULEVARD
LOS ANGELES 15 CALIFORNIA
February 18, 1949

Mother M. Columbanus, Superior General
CONVENT OF ST. LOUIS
Monaghan
Ireland

My dear Mother Columbanus:

This will acknowledge your esteemed letter of February 8, 1949. I give you the answers, herewith, to the questions you inquired about:

1. We would certainly wish to have eight Sisters, but if it is possible to receive only six, we will try to manage. I am asking the Pastor, Father Denis Ginty, to write directly to you regarding this.
2. The travel expenses will be defrayed by the Most Reverend Archbishop.
3. The Archdiocese or the parish will certainly be willing to help defray traveling expenses of a delegation to the General Chapter and the sabbatical vacation of the Sisters.
4. There is no objection to the Sisters receiving gifts "intuitu personae." This does not mean, of course, that there is any general permission to solicit funds for the Community.
5. You may rest assured that the Sisters will be adequately maintained in the Convent; and with the growth of our Archdiocese here, I see no reason why you could not look forward to the establishment of a high school later on.

It is our experience that all the Communities here are in a position and customarily do make returns to their Motherhouse. As I mentioned in my previous letter, we are concerned about the time of the Sisters' arrival, as I understand there can be delays in obtaining the necessary visas.

We are earnestly praying that we will have the privilege of your Community among us.

Very sincerely yours,

+Timothy Manning
Auxiliary Bishop of Los Angeles
Chancellor

Letter 8

Rev. Mother Columbanus
St. Louis Convent, Monaghan.

Reverend dear Mother Columbanus,

His Excellency, Bishop Manning has spoken to me regarding the foundation which you are going to establish here in the archdiocese of Los Angeles.

I have the honor of being the pastor of the parish of the Nativity, one of the parishes which have [sic] more recently been enriched by a parochial school. The need of schools is very grave here, and we are now, throughout the whole archdiocese engaged in a concerted effort to raise funds for the erection of schools in districts where they are *badly needed. The problem is not entirely financial: religious communities to teach in these schools are also being sought. Hence it is a great pleasure to me to know that your order is about to join the army of teachers for our schools.*

Our school was opened in September, 1947, with 450 children enrolled and many others seeking vainly for space in our class-rooms. Last September it was the same story, the number of applicants being far above our capacity. Unfortunately, this is not the only school which is so short of both room and teachers.

Since Bishop Manning told me that he had invited you to take over our school, I am impatiently waiting for your arrival; I earnestly hope you will be able to send enough Sisters to take care of all our present enrollment. I realize that is being greedy, but in this matter I cannot help being greedy, the need being so great. I hope to be able to send you some pictures of our school and convent soon.

Sincerely yours in Christ

(Rev.) Denis Ginty

With the decision to mission sisters to the United States, Mother Columbanus exercised extraordinary generosity. The commitment was a tremendous sacrifice for the individual Sisters of St. Louis and their community. Each sister would earn $50 per month and no pension, resulting in a yearly salary of about $600. Compare this to the £2,000 per year salary (roughly $9,520) paid to the sisters by the Irish government in addition to benefits paid into a pension fund. The critical financial crisis that most religious communities face in the United States today is due to the low salaries and lack of financial planning during these boom years. By 2003 the United States bishops anticipated that retired religious "face more than $20 billion in unfunded retirement liabilities." (See www.usccb.org/nrro for more on the situation of retired sisters.)

The Arrival of the Sisters of St. Louis

The first eight Irish Sisters were led by Mother Columbanus. They arrived by boat in New York from Southampton, England; from there they traveled by train via Chicago and Omaha to Pomona, and then by car to El Monte, California. Sister Maura Byron, SSL, was one of the first missionaries to journey to the United States. In a 2008 interview she offered the following memories of Mother Columbanus, the trip to the United States, and the mission here:

Mother Columbanus was heroic; she was an outstanding figure with great leadership qualities. She had a tremendous sense of humor, and we were in awe of her.

Under the indefatigable leadership of Mother Columbanus, these Sisters of St. Louis set out from their native Ireland to establish a foundation in the rapidly expanding school system of Los Angeles. Their heroic sacrifices typified the generosity of many orders of sisters who built the Catholic schools of the United States.

I always wanted to be a missionary, and I wanted to go to Africa, but my mother did not want me to go and would only let me enter religious life on the condition I wouldn't be a missionary. Soon after I entered she passed away and I felt that now that she was in heaven and would understand my desires and hopes and would be fine with things. So I went to Mother Columbanus, knelt down and requested that I be sent to the African missions. She said, "Well dear, you have jumped the gun. I want you to go to the missions, but not Africa. I want you to go to California; do you know where that is? Go back to the novitiate and look it up on the atlas. We are going to open a mission there." So once I saw it was by Hollywood, I was fine.

When we left on the *Queen Elizabeth* from Southhampton, my father and brother met me at the dock to say goodbye. We had been told and had in our minds that we would never return to Ireland and most likely not see our families again. Mother Columbanus told us that we were not permitted to cry, but the tears came anyway. A few months after my departure, my only brother told my father that he was entering the Holy Ghost Fathers and would be leaving as well; it was very difficult, but he was brave about it. Soon after our arrival, a community chapter decided we could return to visit family; so eight years later I returned and was able to see my father.

It took five days to cross the Atlantic and we were under the watchful eye of Mother Columbanus. We were greeted by the Mayor of New York City who knew our sisters. We were the guests of the Marymount Sisters as well as the Columban Sisters. We were given a tour of the city. Then by train we traveled to Chicago, Omaha, Salt Lake City and then to Pomona. We were welcomed by the pastor and parishioners.

I taught at Nativity for two years. My first class of fifth graders had sixty-five students in it. I remember the first day of class how Sister Claudine and I looked past the gate as the children approached, and we both started crying, but quickly we realized that we had to get on with it! It took twenty years to get my degrees over the summers, but I liked it; I was able to focus on the material I had studied, and I was able to carefully integrate it. I had to study American literature and history since I soon moved to Mater Dei High School in Santa Ana to teach English. I also taught piano and violin lessons on the weekend.

After our arrival ten sisters were sent each year for the next ten years. It has all been a huge blessing for my life; I have loved it all. Mother Columbanus was a visionary, and she had great hopes for our work in the United States. [See appendix A for the letter that Mother Columbanus sent back to Ireland, describing the journey to El Monte, and her impressions of the mission.]

The preceding snapshot of the negotiation and arrival of the Sisters of St. Louis to begin their dedicated service to Catholic education in America is a vivid depiction of a process that was repeated throughout the country with hundreds of different religious communities. Catholic families wanted their children in parish schools. Bishops and pastors were trying to meet these demands. Finding qualified teaching sisters was the challenge. No doubt, each religious community could produce letters from this period echoing the realities of supply and demand that were described by Bishop Manning and Mother Columbanus.

Over the years the Sisters of St. Louis staffed approximately twenty-one different elementary and secondary schools. They sent approximately ten sisters in each subsequent year to labor in the growing educational apostolate in the Archdiocese of Los Angeles. In 1960 Louisville High School for girls opened in Woodland Hills, California, where the sisters also established a provincial house adjacent to the high school. In 2011 this community of sisters was listed in the *Official Catholic Directory* with a membership of fifty-one in the United States. They are known as outstanding educational leaders in the archdiocese and beyond. The next chapter explores how sisters were prepared for their teaching careers.

CHAPTER THREE

~

Preparing the Sisters for Teaching,
Making Sacrifices

In their study *Pioneer Mentoring in Teacher Preparation* (2001), Kevina Keating, CCVI, and Mary Peter Traviss, OP, meticulously captured and documented the process that many teaching sisters experienced when going from the novitiate to the classroom. Vast numbers of young women entered religious life directly after high school and began their two- to three-year formation into the community (the novitiate) before taking vows and receiving their first assignments. There was little or no time for professional academic training, so sisters were often thrown into situations where they were mentored by experienced teaching sisters at their new assignments while working toward their degrees and certifications on Saturdays during the school year and in summer studies.

Hence, an informal professional preparation preceded the formal preparation, which could span many years; this was a highly developed system of mentoring before that term became popular. Some sisters jokingly called this the *twenty-year plan*. Many religious superiors saw the problems inherent in this sink-or-swim model.

One such leader was Holy Cross Sister Madeleva Wolff, who was president of St. Mary's College in Notre Dame, Indiana, from 1934 to 1961. In 1949 Wolff outlined the great need for educating teaching sisters in "The Education of Sister Lucy," a paper presented to the National Catholic Educational Association (NCEA). Ann Carey summarizes the key arguments:

> Sister Madeleva's paper suggested that young sisters who were going to be teachers should receive their baccalaureate degree and teacher certification prior to final profession of vows and prior to being assigned to fulltime

teaching. She acknowledged the problems in trying to attain this ideal—the expense involved in educating a sister before she made a decision to stay in the community before final vows, and the growing pressure for sisters to staff parochial schools—but she insisted that "if we cannot afford to prepare our young sisters for the work of our communities, we should not accept them at all. We should direct them to communities that will prepare them." Sister Madeleva's paper proved to be a major impetus for establishing the Sister Formation Conference.[1]

The Sister Formation Movement worked quickly to establish structure and opportunities for the education of teaching sisters, who were continually challenged by the goal of excellence as a distinguishing mark of all Catholic schools.

Pope Pius XII (1951) paid tribute to the many teaching orders of sisters at a special audience in Rome, but also issued a mild rebuke about the lack of formal preparation for their duties when he stated, "Many of your schools are being described and praised to Us as being very good. But not all. It is Our fervent wish that all endeavor to become excellent."

What may have been lacking in formal preparation was typically compensated by mentoring; practical instructions and advice from the wise and experienced practitioners was shared with junior sisters. Many communities also had school or education supervisors who would visit the schools where their community served. The education supervisor visited each school that was sponsored by a community, and each classroom was observed, evaluated, and advised; these sisters were master teachers and extraordinarily talented.

Keating and Traviss, after interviewing many sisters about their professional experience, summarized the work and impact of the education supervisors in these words:

> The sister-teachers were taught classroom management techniques and methods by the community supervisor in classes, courses, and workshops and were then held accountable on subsequent visits of the community supervisor for what they had learned. Therefore, the ways of the supervisor were faithfully passed along to the younger teachers by the principals, master teachers, and buddies. Often the innovative ideas that were adopted by the community supervisor's congregation were originally her own ideas, or assimilation of ideas she had picked up at meetings and in her own graduate studies, or from interaction with those who held her position in other congregations. These ideas she tailored to the needs of her institute. The community supervisor was consulted about all changes in the schools staffed by her congregation. She suggested which sisters could serve best as principals, and what grade changes should be

made for teachers. Her influence in the annals of American Catholic schools was not overestimated by the sisters.[2]

An illustration of the effectiveness of mentors and supervisors comes from recollections of the Sisters of Charity of Leavenworth. In the 1950s and 1960s the Sisters of Charity of Leavenworth staffed sixty-two elementary schools. During these years, Sister Afra and Sister Baptista were the elementary supervisors but were referred to as "A and B" by the community. Some of the sisters of the community recalled that they worked as a team, while others remembered that they worked individually. What everyone shared in their recollections of these supervisors were the high standards they set and their ability to command deep respect and affection and a bit of intimidation, if not sheer terror, upon the visitations.

No one ever knew when "A and B" would make their visitation to a school. One sister tells the story of being a principal of a school in the Midwest. She had directed the first-grade teacher, whose classroom was nearest the parking lot entrance, to send a messenger to the office as soon as there was a sighting of "A and B" so that an all-points bulletin could caution everyone in the school that the day of scrutiny had arrived.

While these visits would not be considered an ambush, they did bring a certain amount of anxiety to the teaching community. Another sister of this community who was a novice teacher recalled teaching second grade when Sister Baptista suddenly appeared in her room at the very moment her poorest readers were front and center. Sister Baptista grabbed the reader out of the hands of the teacher, saying, "Dear, dear, dear! This book is the fourth in the series, you must use the first. Here's how it should be done!" Sister Baptista proceeded to illustrate the appropriate lesson. The sister noted that Sister Baptista was indeed correct and gave valuable instructions about how to proceed.

Dominican Sister Mary Peter Traviss worked as a community supervisor herself. She described one visit to an elementary school when, upon her arrival, a group of girls playing at recess approached her and one embraced her and said they loved it when she came to visit. When Traviss asked why, the little girl responded that it was only when Traviss visited that the principal was nice to the children.

Smaller communities did not have such directors, but there was plenty of internal support at each local convent. Sister-teachers along with the sister-principal worked on lesson plans together in the convent in the evening. "This was the single best aspect of my training," said one sister. "I lived in the same house as the master teacher, and we met formally every six days but she was always available during each day."[3]

The National Catholic Educational Association developed a department known as Chief Administrators of Catholic Education, or CACE, to continue the work of the community education supervisors; these leaders became our current diocesan superintendents. Commenting on the legacy and era of the sister supervisors, Daniel Curtin, the 2008 executive director of CACE, offered the following observations:

> In the early history of Catholic schools, the role of the diocesan superintendent was a very limited one. Since many Catholic schools were staffed almost entirely by women religious, it was usually the responsibility of the religious community to ensure the quality of the schools under their care. Many religious superiors assigned this task to one of their sisters who served as the community supervisor for schools. It was her responsibility to visit the schools staffed by the order and inspect the teaching methods of the sisters and the accomplishment of the students in their care. Sometimes they were referred to as Sister Supervisors who were usually degreed and had much experience in teaching and administration. These sisters provided an immeasurable contribution to the important role of forming generations of young people in a strong academic program rooted in the Catholic faith. As the role and responsibilities of diocesan superintendents expanded to include closer supervision of Catholic schools in the diocese, the role of the religious communities in the supervision of their schools in dioceses became less and less over time.

Sacrifice as a Way of Life

Communities of sisters met the challenges of training and supervising their many educators, and meanwhile the parishes, too, had particular responsibilities toward these schools. If a parish operated its own grammar school, it did so without any funding from the government, the diocese, or any outside source. The collection basket was the source of financing for all parish activities. It stands to reason that a parish in a more affluent neighborhood would have an easier time meeting the demands of an operating budget.

School parents often tithed a certain amount of money so that their children could attend the parish school. Otherwise, the school was entirely financed with the Sunday collection. Running a school on such slender means was possible because of the contributed services of the sisters, who each received a meager monthly stipend of approximately $50. The sisters were rarely offered health insurance or retirement benefits as part of their employment package.

Sisters often depended upon the generosity and friendship of Catholic hospitals—operated by religious communities of sisters, physicians, and dentists—to contribute their services *gratis* or for a reduced fee. Typically, the parish would provide a car and a convent, and these responsibilities would be outlined in a formal contract.

The contract with the parish was negotiated between the pastor and the religious community's leadership, and a copy was kept on file with the diocese; the forms were fairly standard. A more open type of contract would set out that a community of sisters would provide sisters for the school. Other contracts were more specific, delineating that in exchange for a convent, a car, and a stipend, the community would provide a principal and four sisters. Usually the community's education supervisor negotiated these contracts on behalf of the provincial.

Such a system of contributed services, minimal remuneration for the personnel, and simple living conditions, might seem to some as the image and substance of an ideal society animated by a lively charity and commitment to the common good and love of Jesus the Redeemer. Religious life is certainly premised on such principles, and these would be reflected in the constitutions and governing documents of each religious order or community.

The seven virtues (faith, hope, love, fortitude, justice, prudence, and temperance) provided leaders with perennial sources of material for reflection and practice. Those women who entered religious life embraced a simple life that gave endless opportunities to acknowledge these virtues in word and deed. Difficulties, injustices, or a lack of ordinary comforts could be opportunities for growth along the path of sanctity.

While such themes have a legitimate cadence in the lives of all Christians, these notes were amplified into full symphonies in the lives of women religious. The sisters made extraordinary sacrifices—rarely acknowledged, only occasionally understood, and seldom described in detail. Catholics will often say that they received a good education from the sisters, believing that the sisters sacrificed much for the good of the Church. Much research is needed to uncover what these sacrifices actually entailed.

According to "Sister Kathleen," in one urban school on the east coast, sisters lived in their classrooms while a convent was constructed on the roof of the five-story school. Showers were in the basement of the building, and the school cafeteria doubled as the sisters' refectory when the students were not present. "Sister Timothy" spoke of a convent in the East that had inadequate windows. Newspaper was stuffed around the windows in the winter to keep out the biting cold, and summer offered the challenge of keeping out swarms of flies and mosquitoes because the window screens were in such disrepair. Parish convents relied almost totally on the beneficence of a pastor for any capital improvements. An unfortunate by-product of a spirituality of poverty is that peeling paint, shabby carpet, and dilapidated furniture are not considered important things to address; too often such living conditions were blessed as a virtue, and the sisters were in no position to change this.

Some have jokingly called this the Catholic Church's "seamless garment of cheapness"! This was clearly a takeoff on Joseph Cardinal Bernadin's thesis of the Church's position on all life issues. The "seamless garment of cheapness" means taking the stingy or tawdry path when a generous or aesthetically superior option is available, while cloaking the miserly deed in a spiritual raiment. The quality of workmanship between a convent and rectory was not always identical. In fact, many convents were originally the rectories of a parish that were passed on to the sisters when a new and improved rectory was built for the pastor.

Many convents consisted of tiny bedrooms with thin walls and a small closet, desk, and chair. Most of the parish convents were a mystery to the parishioners, as sisters of this era would not have had open houses. Beyond those who did errands for the sisters, or repair people who made the rounds, or possibly a cook, very few people had access to the convent or would know the condition of the building.

In most Catholic elementary schools, a "food shower" was held each year for the convent, at which time students brought canned and dry goods to school to fill the sisters' larder for the year. Sister Mary Sharon Verbeck, SCL, commented that if meat was ever served, there was enough for each person to have one piece, never seconds. She recalled, "Many nights we went to bed hungry. Once while I was missioned in Wyoming, the mother of one our sisters brought us a bag of groceries every week because she didn't think we were eating enough."

If there were parish merchants, it was a common practice for them to generously offer reduced prices on food and necessities. Families often sent baked goods or fresh produce to the convent. One sister spoke of working in a school in a poor area where the sisters often had but one slice of bologna as dinner for several days at a time. Some pastors saw to it that a freezer was placed in the convent and frequently sent over provisions, and other convents simply did the best they could on their monthly stipends.

Most people would have been shocked to learn of the sacrifices being made by the sisters. Again, there was a legitimate spirituality that spoke to making sacrifices, and the sisters embraced these challenges with earnestness and ardor, but sometimes the degree of severity was not healthy.

"Sister Elizabeth," who was principal in an environment that could easily be described as mentally abusive and un-Christian, describes what kept her going: "You have to focus on your goal as principal and use all your love and energy for those kids."

Often, the days of schools filled with sisters are romanticized, and tales of the harsh realities and sacrifices of the sisters are blithely neglected. Consider the following account by a Catholic schoolteacher who reminisced about her growing awareness of the sacrifice of women religious:

> I have many wonderful memories of Sister Miriam. She was a dear little soul. I had her as a fifth grade teacher at *St. Louise de Marillac* in 1967. The sisters lived in a small home/office structure next door to our school. My mother helped to cook for them and I spent hours in their kitchen doing my homework and smelling fresh cookies being baked. The determination of the sister teachers who persevered through decades of inadequate training and limited resources was most inspiring. It made me pause before complaining of my own inadequacies and be grateful for the support and virtually limitless resources I have available in my classes. I was reminded of Sister Miriam, my fifth grade teacher, and her stories of life in the school convent. The sisters had only the bare necessities and did without items we take for granted today. I remember one day, finding her at her desk gluing her false tooth back in place with Elmer's glue because there was no money for a dentist, and I stood there with a mouthful of braces. These women were true disciples who taught us more than academics. They taught us to think, and to hope, and to have faith when all seemed hopeless.

This sister, like many others, sacrificed so that parish families could provide for their children what she was unable to obtain for herself—something as common as regular dental care.

CHAPTER FOUR

~

From the Motherhouse
to the Classroom

While the sacrifices sisters made may be little known, both the culture of Catholic schools and their style of discipline from the pre-conciliar period are legendary. One must consider that many classrooms were filled with anywhere from thirty to sixty students; it was not unusual to hear reports of even higher enrollments. Many of the sisters who were interviewed reported that the pastor would present children to be enrolled even after school was in session without any extra books, desks, or supplies.

Such numbers demanded clear rules, less chaos reign and eclipse any kind of meaningful learning experience. But beyond the good order of a school lies a hidden pattern that informed the school culture, and it was that of the novitiate experience of the sisters.

When young women entered religious life at the congregation's motherhouse, they began an intense period of discernment and preparation that generally lasted between two and three years, depending on the community and its governing constitutions. During this period the primary question to be answered by the candidate and the community was whether this way of life was a good fit.

This question, which could be posed in many ways, became the background music that accompanied sister candidates during the process of socialization into the community's life and customs. Formal classes were taught on the Catholic faith, along with the history of the community, and the vows of poverty, chastity, and obedience that the novices would one day profess.

Sister Antonine Signorelli, ASCJ, is pictured here in 1938 at Sacred Heart Private School in the Bronx.

In addition to classes, the days were punctuated with times for praying the Liturgy of the Hours in common, Mass, spiritual reading and reflection, manual work, silence, and recreation. Bells would often be used to alert everyone to the next activity. Much of the day was spent in silence, so that the novice could tune out distractions and focus more upon the internal movements of the Spirit. It was in this novitiate experience that a deep sense of respect for the ways of religious life was instilled—a respect for one's superiors and leaders, community members, friends, benefactors, and daily routines and rituals. The sisters found this cultivated the virtue of respect essential to the life and spirit of their schools as well.

A profound respect for the dignity of the individual emerges in the educational philosophy of the sisters, but its foundation rests in a respect for authority, traditions, teachings, and property. The sisters made special efforts to inculcate this attitude of respect in their students, with the hope that it would pass beyond the schoolroom and be reflected in the students' attitudes toward their faith, families, church and civic leaders, and school and neighborhood property. Making a pencil mark in a book or on a desk was no small misdemeanor. Students needed a sense of stewardship, as these items would be used by many others in the future.

A kindergarten report card (figure 4.1), designed especially for Catholic schools in the late 1950s early 1960s, notes the following understandings and extensions of respect under the category of Christian Social Living: "I am polite, I obey, I know my prayers, I follow directions, I am careful of school things, I play nicely, I listen attentively."

These became the bedrock of a Catholic education. These moral goals taught to youngsters were a reflection of the community formation sisters received in the novitiate and lived as adults in their apostolic convents. Keating and Traviss cited evidence of this:

> In large measure, the schedule of the school likewise matched that of the convent. Holy days were holidays; visitation from the Mother Superior usually meant an inspection of the school and a free day for the students; school doors were locked for the beginning of the afternoon prayers in the convent. In fact, several sisters spoke of teaching as an extension of their common life.[1]

"Sister Joan" commented, "Our lives were steeped in so many customs and traditions that we simply carried these into the schools. As a young sister, you were being initiated into the school's culture, and there were many senior members of the community handing onto you the school's tradition." With the charism of the community animating the leaders of the schools, it comes as no surprise that traditions in the classroom could trace their genealogy through the parish convent directly to the novitiate experience at the motherhouse. When one considers how swiftly young women moved from the novitiate to the classroom, this connection is easy to understand.

This spiritual legacy that was a part of the culture of the schools was simply taken for granted. The way a Catholic school looked, its web of relationships, its rituals, and the manner in which business was conducted defined in the hearts and minds of all people what a Catholic school was about.[2] Sisters who taught during that time speak of their congregation's schools as having a unique educational philosophy that typified the school's climate and culture.

Figure 4.1. Kindergarten Report Card

Community Culture and the Apostles
of the Sacred Heart of Jesus

An example of these distinct congregational cultures can be found in the Apostles of the Sacred Heart of Jesus, founded by Clelia Merloni in 1894 at Viareggio, Italy. In 1963 there were 267 professed sisters; the community in 2011 counted 132 members serving in its U.S. Province. The Apostles describe their beginnings and mission on their website:

> In June 16, 1902, six Apostle Missionaries from the Italian Province sailed from Genoa to Boston, Massachusetts. The Sisters were sent to assist the emigrants who had abandoned Italy in search of a livelihood in the United States.

Figure 4.1. (*continued*)

Within a short time these sisters had gathered about 200 children from the area and organized Christian Doctrine classes for them.

By 1905, fifteen other sisters had come from Italy. A building in the Orient Heights section was purchased for a novitiate for young sisters and for a small hospital.

In 1906 we branched out to the Diocese of Hartford, becoming established in New Haven, Connecticut. Over the years, we Apostles began ministering in other States: Missouri, Pennsylvania, New York, Illinois, Michigan, Rhode Island, Florida, New Jersey and California. Since 1998, the U.S. Province has also had a mission in Taiwan.

Although education is the primary apostolate of the Province, sisters are also involved in social work, legal assistance, nursing and health care, pastoral ministry, after school programs, elderly day care and other works of charity.

The Provincial House has been located in Hamden, CT since 1953 on a 125-acre property known as Mount Sacred Heart. Formerly known as "Cherry Hill," the parcel is one of the highest spots in the surrounding area. Purchased from the family of Manley Chester in 1946, reminders of the Chester estate remain: orchards, magnificent trees, and the family's stately home, presently used by sisters in Formation.[3]

The Apostles of the Sacred Heart of Jesus (ASCJ) speak of a sense of hospitality and familial warmth that has always been part of their educational philosophy. They strive to know each school family personally and build a relationship with them, which creates a connection between the community and the family that lasts long after students graduate. Even in the days of community newsletters and websites, sisters serving in parishes and schools are the news source on the health, assignments, and updates of sisters who served a parish and its school in the past.

It should be noted that before Vatican II, many communities had customs that governed communication of the sisters, and news about sisters who once served the parish and school traveled through more formal channels. Some sisters had to have permission to write a letter to family members, and more often than not, all incoming and outgoing mail was subject to prescreening by a superior.

The Apostles, however, were committed to establishing strong ties. While this attachment between parishioners and sisters—emerging from their emphasis on hospitality—was generally seen as positive, it also reaped its share of inappropriate expectations and demands.

For example, one Apostle recalled a group of school parents who complained at an open meeting with leadership about the community's assignment of sisters to other schools and ministries when they felt their school should be a priority and insisted more sisters should be assigned there. This clear overstepping of boundaries on the part of the school parents into the internal governance of the community was one of the undesired negative outcomes of the sisters' mission to be welcoming and inviting and establish bonds with the people they served.

Overall, though, this community has successfully distinguished itself by making people feel that they are a genuine and important part of the sisters' lives. The sisters have made themselves available to parishioners seeking counsel and are looked to as spiritual leaders. Their commitment to their charism of welcome is manifested in their presence in parishes, care for school families, involvement with those who request assistance, and all the typical encounters that take place in parishes and parish schools.

Sister Assumpta Papa, ASCJ, rehearses with the Boys Choir of St. Ambrose Parish on the Hill in St. Louis, Missouri. In addition to teaching duties, many sisters had extra duties as piano instructors, choir directors, organists, and religion teachers to parish children attending public schools.

Community Culture and the Sisters of Charity of Leavenworth

Other communities cultivated different hallmarks of distinction. The Sisters of Charity of Leavenworth was founded in 1858 by Mother Xavier Ross, who had been a member of the Sisters of Charity of Nazareth, Kentucky. In 1963 the community had one thousand members; the 2011 statistics place community membership at 306.[4] In 1858, sixteen sisters journeyed to Leavenworth, a military outpost in the Kansas territory on the Missouri River. They were met with a "scene of rioting, border warfare, illegal elections, and insecure titles to property."

> Despite these circumstances, the sisters began to teach regular classes and to nurse the sick in private homes until they opened the first civilian hospital in Kansas (1863). . . . During the sisters' 1st decade in Kansas membership in the community increased; they established a novitiate, orphanage, hospital, two academies, and three day schools. . . . During the 20th century the sisters

extended their work into Missouri, Illinois, Wyoming, California, Oklahoma, and Nebraska. On the same campus as the motherhouse the sisters staffed St. Mary's College [now university].[5]

Throughout their history, the Sisters of Charity of Leavenworth's ministries have focused on health and education, executed, according to the sisters, with a common sense approach of practicality and making due with limited resources. As reported by the sisters, the distinct and distinguished character of their schools flowed from their community's culture and charisms, which were rooted in the spirituality of St. Vincent de Paul. Like St. Vincent, whose solicitude for and service to the poor are nearly synonymous with his name, the sisters have always had a special commitment to the poor and disadvantaged.

"Sister Esther" noted, "Our tradition was to serve the economically disadvantaged who lack options, especially in quality education. I think we have traditionally offered such students a quality education for the whole person, and the basis of this is faith."

"Sister Mary Jean" commented that the community's concern extended even to meeting some of the material needs of families:

> Often enough in a parish, it was the sisters who learned first of a family's hardships. I recall giving money, getting groceries delivered, sharing our own food, and purchasing clothing. We often made connections between the resources and those in need, but just as often, we provided the help from our own resources, such as they were.

Those who work with small children know it is not unusual for them to report in school all the delicate issues unfolding at home. So it seems logical that the teaching sisters were often the first to learn about a parent losing a job or about other stresses on a family.

CHAPTER FIVE

~

Working with Pastors

No matter what the varying charism and culture of the community might be, the framework of authority was the same for each school. Once the sisters were established in parishes, the superiors of the order then dealt with the pastors regarding the supply and demand of teaching sisters. This was (and continues to be) a less than perfect arrangement considering the lack of preparation parish priests received to lead schools. In addition, at least as far back as the nineteenth century, a parish depended completely upon the motherhouse to supply teachers for its elementary school:

> A necessary prerequisite for the establishment of Catholic schools was the availability of teachers. By the middle of the century, teaching became the preserve of women, and Catholics were fortunate to have available a large pool of women religious sisters to staff the schools.[1]

According to the 1983 Code of Canon Law that governs the Catholic Church, the pastor is ultimately the leader of an elementary school, since the school is a ministry of his parish; he is responsible for leading and managing the school. With the possible exception of a pastoral experience of teaching catechism in an elementary school while in the seminary, there is essentially no professional preparation in the seminary for assuming the role of managing a school. Diocesan offices may offer some continuing educational experiences for pastors, but the lion's share of a priest's preparation to work with a school consists of *on-the-job training*.

It must be clearly stated that, although an inimical relationship between pastors and elementary schools is not the norm, clerical leadership and support for Catholic schools is not always evident.[2] In February 2006 while giving a keynote address on Catholic Education at Loyola Marymount University, then Milwaukee archbishop Timothy Dolan stated that the time had come to "re-evangelize the clergy" toward promoting Catholic schools. The audience, which was composed primarily of Catholic school teachers, administrators, and leaders from the Archdiocese of Los Angeles, broke into spontaneous, loud, and sustained applause. The archbishop had clearly struck a responsive chord, which many of us involved in Catholic education have similarly witnessed.

A study conducted in 2004 offers some hopeful evidence that support for Catholic schools may be growing among clergy. The study sought to understand the attitudes of seminarians toward being assigned to parishes with elementary schools. These seminarians were in their final years of preparation for ordination and had had some experience with various pastoral responsibilities at the parish level. Moreover, they were being socialized into the presbyterate and exposed to a wide range of priests with diverse opinions.

Two important findings emerged from the study. First, the seminarians saw the parish school as a valuable evangelical presence and vehicle to build community. Second, the seminarians cited the priests they knew and admired as strong advocates of Catholic schools.

This is good news because, in the words of Mission San Jose Dominican Sister Mary Peter Traviss, an acclaimed scholar and expert in Catholic education, "The pastor makes or breaks the assignment." An interesting aside to illustrate the importance of the pastor's role in the sisters' success at an elementary school: during the course of interviews with the sisters and laypeople for this book, each respondent brought up their relationship with the pastor, even though this question was not a part of the interview. Traviss also recalls that whenever there were meetings of elementary school principals, the first topic of conversation was the pastor.

A pattern began to emerge as the various pastors were described, descriptions that ranged from angelic to diabolical. Numerous stories were told of kindnesses, consistent support, friendship, and collegiality offered by priests. Unfortunately, abundant stories were also told of greed, rudeness, and total lack of Christian charity.

Eventually, four models were developed to describe the pastor of a parish with an elementary school; perhaps the distinctions made here may seem a bit superficial, but they are offered as a way to understand the past, provide hope for the future, and begin a long overdue conversation.

Models of Pastors

Father Hostile

At one end of the spectrum is Father Hostile, who basically resents the school and has openly confessed he would prefer not to be assigned to a parish with a school. He sees the school as a colossal drain on the limited finances of the parish. This diversion of funds effectively limits all other creative initiatives for the sake of a small number of parish families, many of whom, in his view, do not practice their faith in any meaningful way but are exploiting the school.

This pastor comes only to necessary functions, and he does so reluctantly. The principal is often on pins and needles trying to figure out how to placate this pastor. He does not offer support to the principal, faculty, staff, or school families.

Father Schizophrenia

The second pastoral model is Father Schizophrenia. This pastor accepts the presence of a school, but his support is unpredictable. At times he attends school functions and seems to be a great supporter of the school, but he can be difficult when dealing with the principal and staff. The wider community has a positive perception of his leadership, but the principal, faculty, and staff paint a very different picture. He will on occasion erratically entangle himself in the leadership of the school, especially regarding finances or ad-ministrative minutiae.

This is the pastor who may heap praise upon a teacher or principal one day, but then not be willing to renew his or her contract because of newly found flaws. This is not an unheard-of tactic, though hardly ethical or just, for meeting an operating budget. Longtime employees have a higher salary to meet, and it is much less expensive to hire a freshly minted BA than meet the salary requirements of an MA with years of experience.

Father Laissez-faire

The third model is Father Laissez-faire. This pastor accepts the school's presence and will dutifully be available, but he sees himself in an auxiliary role, and not really as a leader of the school community. He is attentive to meeting the needs of the school's finances. He attends all necessary func-tions perfunctorily as part of his pastoral work. He has clearly empowered the principal to run the school and is supportive of this person as the educational expert; he will always support the principal, but he may be aloof to faculty and staff. He accepts the school as an integral part of the parish's mission and vitality within the community, but he offers no vision or inspiration.

Father Engaged

The final model is Father Engaged, who sees himself as a leader of the school and is enthusiastic about the school's presence. He collaborates in meeting the financial needs of the school; he recognizes his strengths and challenges and seeks the wisdom of other experts in various fields. This pastor is regularly present at the school through various activities. He knows the faculty, staff, and children. He has empowered the principal, but he works as a member of a team. This pastor sees the school as an integral value to the mission of the parish and the good of the neighborhood.

Table 5.1. Models of Pastors with Parish Schools

	Father Hostile	Father Schizophrenia	Father Laissez-faire	Father Engaged
Overall attitude toward the school	Sees the school as a drain on limited resources	Vacillates depending upon mood and audience	Sees the school as part of the big picture of the parish	Recognizes the school as an evangelizing agent
Mission	Anachronistic relic	Resigned that it serves a purpose	Nonjudgmental	Sees the school as an asset in all ways
Relationship with school principal	Constantly tense	Anxious	Empowers but can be distant	Collegial and supportive
Relationship with school staff and students	Aloof	Apprehensive	Attitudinally supportive, but remote	Amiable and cooperative
Relationship with school families	Formal	Cordial	Encouraging	Sociable
Personal involvement with the school	Unenthusiastic	Erratic	Perfunctory	Regularly present

The four pastor models offered here, while undoubtedly needing further exploration and validation, serve as reference points for the narratives that follow. "Sister Elizabeth" offered this comment about the kinds of pastors one might have found (and may continue to find) working with an elementary school:

> It is true, (A) the formal training of priests in school administration and management, though minimal, is extremely important—but, equally important is

(B) the pastor's personal attitude, concern, interest, support and understanding of the school's mission and its long-term effect on the church at large. (A) and (B) are not synonymous. To self-educate (on the job training) is one task. To self-motivate is another.

This insight not only offers a realistic assessment of the state of priestly preparation for working with schools, but also serves as an appeal to bring decency and humility to the task, no matter what the pastor's formal preparation may be.

Aware that the relationship between the pastor and school was foundational for the success of the school, some sisters registered protests with the diocese and bishops over priests being assigned to parishes with schools when they were clearly hostile to the project; some priests' senates made and passed recommendations to their bishop that belligerent priests should never be inflicted on a parish with a school. Unfortunately, such recommendations were not always followed, particularly as priestly vocations began to diminish.

The comment above in (B) is also a prophetic reminder that in the United States, Catholic schools have been and remain one of the most valuable means for evangelization and discipleship, a truth that Father Andrew Greeley has repeatedly studied, demonstrated, and shouted from the rooftops for more than fifty years in his research and numerous books (Greeley, 1998, 2005 [*Priests: A Calling in Crisis*; "The Treason of the Clerks"], 2008; Greeley et al., 1976).

Unfortunately, some of the more prosperous parishes have schools, and as clergy are promoted, their views about the schools are not always their primary concern when accepting a transfer. Now, with the desperate shortage of priestly vocations within the Church, the problem with assignments is more a case of being fortunate enough to find a breathing cleric to keep a parish base covered. Parishes with a pastor and a few curates are indeed rare. Many older Catholics can recall larger parishes that had a staff of priests serving the people; at those same parishes today, one overworked and hectored shepherd is probably trying to keep the feisty flock together.

In addition to their lack of management and administration training, during the boom years, many newly ordained diocesan priests were assigned to teach in diocesan high schools along with their parish assignments. They had no formal preparation for this task, and they generally taught religion. What they lacked in training, they often made up for in youth and enthusiasm. If a young priest was assigned with a seasoned pastor, he might gain some effective skills through this mentoring system, but if he was with a pastor from one of the negative models, he might be in a learning void.

One of the parish priest's duties was a weekly round to visit various class-rooms for catechism and interaction with the children. Most people have fond memories of these encounters. The priest typically interrupted the usual class schedule and provided a change of pace for the students as well as the teacher. It is important to realize that the relationship of the religious order with parishes often depended upon the rapport that the teaching sisters had with the pastor. An engaged pastor would garner good press at the mother-house, while a tyrant would try the patience of a saint.

Conversely, good pastors most likely had their share of challenges with difficult religious. This relationship, which could be good, neutral, or occa-sionally toxic, provided the context for supplying sisters to the schools. One corrective to all this when vocations were at their unprecedented peak was that most pastors and most principals were assigned to a parish for no more than six years, which meant consistent renewal for the parish and school.

Every six years or so, a new principal was needed for the parish school and would be assigned to the school under the direction of the community's education supervisor, the provincial, and possibly a leadership team. This arrangement provided renewal as well as challenges for the principals, the teaching sisters, the pastors, and the parish and school families.

Lay Teachers: Partners with the Sisters

During the years from approximately 1945 to 1980, the schools were staffed primarily with sisters, though not exclusively. Many young laywomen who had been educated to be elementary school teachers also joined the sisters in the teaching apostolate. With motivation that paralleled the sisters' desires to serve God and the Church, these women often attended Catholic col-leges or junior colleges, often on the grounds of the motherhouse, that were sponsored by various religious communities.[3]

Among the many communities that sponsored such institutions were the Sisters of St. Joseph, the Sisters of Mercy, various branches of the Benedic-tine Sisters, Dominican Sisters, Sisters of the Blessed Virgin Mary, and the scores of communities that now form the Vincentian religious tradition, such as the Daughters of Charity and various groups of the Sisters of Charity.

If a girl attended a particular high school sponsored by a community, there was most likely a strong push for college-bound young women to seriously consider the religious community's college. Frequently these colleges would offer scholarships to girls from the high schools affiliated with the order. Naturally many of these young women were encouraged to consider a reli-gious vocation to the community as well.

The presence of these lay colleagues in the elementary school would prepare the next generation of leaders in Catholic schools because when the sisters were no longer available to fill the leadership positions of principal, the pastor usually turned to one of these lay teachers to assume the role.

As Father Denis Ginty's letter (Letter 8, chapter 2, pages 23–24) to Mother Columbanus noted, he wanted as many sisters as possible, mainly because the prospect of paying a salary for a lay teacher, though a fraction of what such a teacher would have earned in a public school, was still a considerable amount of money for a parish.

Dolan points out, "By the early 20th century, sisters generally received an annual salary of about $200, or one third less than female public-school teachers and one half that received by teaching brothers. Many times pastors failed to pay the full salary."[4] So most parishes welcomed the generous educational bargain that the sisters provided.

Many of these laywomen were likely to marry or were married and had perhaps begun to raise families. They might have taught a few years as a single person, then got married, and subsequently stepped out of the classroom to raise their children. When the children reached school age, many of these teachers returned to teach and work in the schools. More often than not, their salary did not constitute the sole income for their family and was often used for extras in the family. If it were not for the income of their spouses, they could never have afforded to work in a Catholic school. Lay educational leaders often speak with admiration and appreciation for the sisters with whom they worked; many significant, life-long friendships were established and many of these continue to endure. These lay educators also noted some practices that by today's standards seem peculiar or quaint.

In some of the schools there was often a small break room for the lay teachers and a dining room that was considered part of the convent's cloister and was open only to the sisters. Most of the major decisions about the school were made by the sisters; the lay staff had very little input.

For example, in one particular school the first day of Christmas vacation was set very close to December 25 to accommodate sisters' meetings and travel schedules to the motherhouse. The lay staff, all mothers, lamented not having a few days more before Christmas to focus upon the needs of their families and organize the holidays with less stress.

Noting these quirky exceptions, the lay teachers felt that they and sisters shared equally in their extra duties on the playground or in the lunchroom. In fact, everyone looked to the sisters for leadership in conducting the school and setting its standards. They looked to the sisters to handle various celebrations and traditions (such as October and May devotions in honor of Mary), to determine how children entered the church and behaved during Mass, to choose which prayers would be learned, and to organize all the large and small events that made up the life of a parish school. Again, many of these traditions were imported from the novitiate experience and further augmented through the mentoring system that was in place inside the convent; the lay colleagues absorbed all these lessons.

Today in many Catholic schools, from elementary through institutions of higher education, there are endless discussions and presentations on the mission and identity of the school. In the post–World War II period, the mission permeated everything that was done. Those first lay leaders were deeply imbued with the Catholic culture of the school, though perhaps not always as well versed in articulating it. The sisters were mentoring them for leadership roles—preparing them for the day when the sisters would say farewell. The roles of leadership would serve as a transition from a period when the sisters' presence dominated to a new era when the exact opposite would be the case.

CHAPTER SIX

~

Changes in Religious Life Lead to Departures

Among the events and concerns of American and Catholic society during the 1960s and 1970s were Vatican II (with its spirit of change and renewal), the war on poverty, the civil rights movement to end racial discrimination, the peace movement to end the Vietnam War, the rise of feminist ideologies and the women's movement for equal rights, Latin American liberation movements, concern about the environment, protests against police brutality and civil unrest in major urban areas, disturbances on university campuses, the Watergate scandal (which cast doubt on the ethics in government and fed into a pervasive mistrust and suspicion of most institutions and figures of authority), and the white Catholic migration to the suburbs.

All of these major events had a direct or indirect impact on Catholic education. Many of these winds of change greatly influenced communities of women religious. Vatican II asked religious communities to rediscover their charism and the vision of their founders and charged them to renew their constitutions. They were to do so first in accord with current Church documents and, second, in anticipation of an updated Code of Canon Law to be promulgated in 1983.

As a result of their study and renewal, many communities saw ministerial needs outside the traditional educational, health care, and social service systems, and they opted to pursue these new apostolates. Many communities rediscovered and re-embraced their founders' emphasis on serving those in poverty. Many sisters who were not really drawn to working in schools finally saw an opportunity to find a better professional fit as social workers, pastoral associates, chaplains, and advocates for the poor. Many also sought advanced degrees for professional occupations that required different skill sets than those of teachers. The renewal of religious life that was mandated by Vatican II, the course it took in the United States, and its cultural context would have a profound, and in many ways deleterious, effect upon Catholic schools.

The complex web of changes in women's religious communities is not the focus of this book. What is clear is that these changes resulted in dramatically fewer sisters. Because that impact has been so significant for the schools, a short review of those changes is called for:

- Unusually high numbers of women entered religious life in the 1940s, 1950s, and 1960s. When the number of entrants reverted to historical norms in subsequent decades, the decrease was felt acutely.
- Increased professional opportunities for women, beginning in the 1970s, gave young women more options. They could pursue apostolic works without joining a religious order.
- The changes in religious life following Vatican II decrees created turmoil in some communities, resulting in members leaving and others lacking the enthusiasm required to recruit new members.
- Religious garb was reevaluated, and many communities chose to dress like the people they served to better identify with them and reduce barriers. An unintended consequence was lower visibility.
- As communities adopted new ministries, moving into apartments to be closer to those they served, communal life diminished.
- With fewer unifying forces—same ministry, same convent, same clothing—many communities suffered an erosion of their identity.
- Within the Catholic population, the level of engagement in the Church decreased, making the pool of young adults attracted to ministry smaller.
- Catholic families became smaller since the 1970s, and parents became much less likely to encourage their children to pursue religious life or priestly vocations.

The landmark 2009 study *Recent Vocations to Religious Life*, conducted by the Center for Applied Research in the Apostolate (CARA) on behalf of the National Religious Vocation Conference, was designed to identify and to understand the characteristics of the men and women who are coming to religious life today and the characteristics of the religious institutes and societies that are attracting and successfully retaining new members. It found that new members were more ethnically and culturally diverse and possessed a strong desire for prayer, communal living, and Catholic identity. In addition, while many communities are not receiving new members, among the Millennial generation (those born from 1982 to 2001), there has been an uptick of interest in life as a sister, brother, or priest. Also, younger religious are much less interested than their forebears in the controversies of Vatican II.[1]

The current state of religious life for women's communities involves a wide spectrum of lifestyles and ministries. The singular focus on health care and education no longer exists. Furthermore, the number of new entrants is much smaller today than in the heyday of Catholic schools—a period of atypical growth. As Mother Mary Clare Millea, ASCJ, head of the Vatican-sponsored Apostolic Visitation of Women Religious in the United States, stated in a 2010 interview, "That was a very unusual and unique peak in the number of vocations in the 1950s. After the pioneering and the struggling times, part of it is that we built so many institutions. Those institutions met so many young people and influenced their lives, causing them to join and to become a part of that. That was a passing phenomenon, and many of the institutions have been taken over by other people so capably."[2]

The Paths of Renewal

How the various congregations of sisters took up the task of rewriting their constitutions and implementing their internal renewal project is not the focus of this book, but a few observations are appropriate since the most visible and chief casualties of this renewal was the harmful impact on Catholic schools and the diminishment of the numbers of teaching sisters. Many have tried to describe this history of sisters in the United States and their inestimable contribution to building the Catholic Church in this country with varying degrees of success and accuracy.

Two books deserve consideration on the topic. The first, John Fialka's *Sisters: Catholic Nuns and the Making of America* (2003), gives a thorough and inspired history of sisters, utilizing the example of the Sisters of Mercy in the United States before and after Vatican II; his excellent description serves as a template for the establishment of ministries and the path of renewal that many other orders took. In the second book, journalist Ann Carey has carefully documented an excellent historical perspective of the paths of renewal taken by various communities in her book *Sisters in Crisis: The Tragic Unraveling of Women's Religious Communities* (1997).

Utilizing the archives of the Leadership Conference of Women Religious, numerous interviews, and all the relevant Church documents, Carey provided an indispensable explanation of how the changes led to a widespread plummeting of new vocations, the diminution of the workforce, and a growing dissatisfaction with the educational apostolate as a corporate or personal choice for many sisters. Undoubtedly, the perspective and interpretations of this book may be debated, but the substantiation of its realities remains irrefutable and part of the historical record. Perhaps the historical proximity to these events prevents a calm and honest assessment of the various directions renewal took, due to the vested interest and the fierce ideological allegiance of its living architects. Many Catholics who lived through these times of renewal have very strong feelings and opinions about the transformation of religious life and the seeming collective trauma it was experiencing.

Many who were sympathetic to the changes would applaud the "change-oriented" sisters, as Carey describes them. These sisters sought a radical break with the old structure and its semi-monastic lifestyle. The change-oriented sisters often disregarded the documents and directives of the Church, dismissing them as retroactive and fearing capitulation to what they perceived as a corrupt and patriarchal system. Instead, they sought inspiration from within the community's wisdom figures, the fields of psychology and political science, and various spiritual sources to renew their constitutions and life.

Many Catholics were dismayed to see the disappearance of the "traditional" sisters. The traditional sisters themselves also embraced change with an eagerness to update religious life. The traditional sisters took a more gradual approach to revitalization and used the documents and the directives of the Church as their guides in renewal. The presence of the traditional sisters was generally identifiable, though not always, through the wearing of an updated habit. The habit or religious clothing remains for many a very positive and powerful symbol, though for others, it is controversial and represents all that is wrong with the Church and its attitude toward women. Clearly, it does not make the wearer better or holier than anyone who does not wear it, but it does send a message, and many would say that it is a positive message.

Much to the consternation of the change-oriented sisters, the historical record shows that the more traditional orders, estimated at about 20 percent of religious communities in the United States today, are the ones that experienced stability and some growth during and after Vatican II. Traditional orders typically, but not always, wear a modified habit chosen by the order, live in community more often than not, share a clearly identifiable and common apostolate, and have a communal prayer life. The future of religious life for women in the United States may be with these orders of traditional sisters.

Carey (1997) cited the research of sociologist Roger Finke. He found that "the decline in communal living, the loss of distinctive dress, and the increase in individual autonomy all increase nongroup activity." And as sisters spent less time with their community, they received fewer rewards from the community's social networks, which also made it easier for them to leave religious life. Finke also found that group solidarity is important for supporting a member's religious commitment, because members of the group offer support and confirmation to one another. But, "as members reduce their investment in community activities and increase nongroup activities, the group is less capable of supporting the extremely high levels of religious commitment associated with religious orders."

This theory explains why traditional religious orders are more successful in attracting recruits, according to Finke. Since membership demands are high for religious life, the order must offer the member "a religious lifestyle that is distinctive from that of the laity." But Finke also observed that a traditional religious order does not mean a pre–Vatican II order, for there are successful orders that have heeded the call of Vatican II to return to the spirituality of their founders in a creative way while still retaining the strict demands of common life.[3]

Perhaps there are two points of agreement among the diversity of interpreting this period of renewal:

1. There is a shared melancholy about the widespread diminishment of women religious as a presence and force for good. The disappearance of sisters from parishes, schools, and other Catholic institutions was a distressing development in the contemporary Church.
2. There is no possibility of retreat or second-guessing for either the change-oriented sisters or the traditional sisters, and there is at times an unfortunate tension between the two groups.

Sadly, this topic is quite contentious and varying theories abound, but what is clear is that young people continue to be attracted to religious life. The expression of that life has taken two distinct paths, particularly among women religious. Cardinal James Hickey of Washington, DC, characterized these differences in *Origins*, a special report to a Vatican commission established to understand the impact of renewal on religious vocations. In this address he stated,

At the present time, I see two basic orientations with regard to religious life: The first stresses mission and ministry; the second stresses consecration and community. I hasten to add that neither group intends to emphasize one aspect of religious life to the exclusion of the other.

A. The focus on mission seems characteristic of the majority of religious institutes of men and women in the United States. Since the council, these institutes have stressed the importance of being in the midst of the world in order to address its needs. Consequently, the external structures of religious life are de-emphasized with a view toward immersion in ministry. Indeed some religious describe the fundamental purpose of religious life as "community for mission." Small communities or living alone in apartments is sometimes chosen as a way of drawing close to those who are to be served. Choosing one's ministry in consultation with superiors replaces direct assignment. In some few cases religious engage in works not specifically related to the church.

Some institutes have turned from corporate commitments such as teaching and health care in order to work on social justice issues. They perceive a need to become more politically effective in both church and civic communities. Many religious are convinced they are developing new forms of religious life while at the same time living in a manner consonant with membership in an approved religious institute.

B. A second approach focuses on consecration through the vows as a value in itself and as a basis for community apostolate. This view represents a smaller percent of institutes, sometimes described as "traditional" or "conservative." Some groups, though not all, draw a steady stream of candidates. Nevertheless, such groups often feel they are a minority whose views are not adequately considered. They see continuity with the past as necessary for future growth. They look to the magisterium and their own traditions to determine future directions. These groups believe religious consecration is nurtured by the external structures of conventual living; they maintain and emphasize the centrality of common life, common prayer, the religious habit and community-based ministries. The role of the superior remains fundamental to their notion of religious obedience. Above all, these religious stress the transcendent nature of the consecrated religious life even as they serve human needs here and now.[4]

Open-Placement System and School Staffing

One internal change in religious communities—open placement—ushered in after Vatican II, had a significant impact on Catholic school staffing. Unlike the past method of institutional commitments to parishes with sisters being assigned to various posts within a school as needed, open placement was a growing trend by which communities allowed individual sisters to find positions. The sisters were then missioned to those assignments in the name of the community; hence, the institutional commitment of an order to a parish was decentralized by allowing each sister to choose her ministry in dialogue with the congregation's leadership and approval.[5]

Sometimes a community would receive requests for their sisters for various jobs, and after approval would circulate these job openings among the members through the congregation's newsletters or other means of communication. Sisters, in some communities, could also opt out of an assignment or choose their own assignments. When the request for a change in assignment, need for retirement, or desire to pursue professional growth came along, the last sister at a school effectively terminated the relationship between the school and the congregation, since the community no longer had the ability to supply further staff. For many congregations, the open-placement system created a slow attrition, perhaps barely noticeable to the average parishioner.

Hypothetical Parish of St. Philip the Apostle

The trend of withdrawing from schools took place along a spectrum. One pole, or point of initiative for withdrawal, is that of the congregation's initiative. At the other end of the spectrum is that of the individual's initiative.

Prior to Vatican Council II, all congregations would have exercised decision-making through the leadership of a provincial and her team of advisors. In this model, congregations would have institutional commitments to parishes, and sisters would be missioned to these schools in the name of the community.

It might be instructive to consider a theoretical case study of the last sisters to serve at the parish school of St. Philip the Apostle over a fifteen-year period from 1965 to 1980: Sisters Anne, Renee, Lucy, Janet, George, Rita, José, Catherine, Bernadette, and Maria. A hypothetical example of the transition from a congregation's withdrawal to the open-placement method will illustrate a common scenario.

In 1965, St. Philip's, a parish elementary school (K–8) with 425 students, had seven sisters and two lay teachers, with the principal also teaching eighth grade. In 1967 the sister principal, Sister Anne, became a full-time principal and hired an eighth-grade lay teacher. In 1968 Sister Renee left religious life and was not replaced by another sister.

In 1969 Sister Lucy, who had been at the school for four years, was transferred to another school, and Sister Janet took her place. In 1970, Sister George, who was quite elderly, retired to the motherhouse and was not replaced by another sister.

Also in 1970, Sister Bernadette was elected to a full-time leadership position at the provincial house. In 1971 Sister Catherine joined the community's mission in Haiti and was not replaced by a sister. During the school year of 1973–1974, Sister José became very sick in November and would not likely return until the spring of that year, if at all. She was replaced by a layperson, and now two sisters remained in the school.

At the end of the 1973–1974 school year, Sister Janet left St. Philip's to enter a clinical pastoral education program to be certified as a hospital chaplain; she would be replaced by a lay teacher. This arrangement left Sister Anne as the only member of her community serving in the parish school for the 1974–1975 school year. During these years of the early 1970s, the community was undergoing changes in its governance as it adapted the decrees of Vatican II.

The congregation chose to use the open placement of sisters and was now allowing sisters more freedom to pursue other ministries besides teaching, nursing, and administration within those apostolates. Not only were sisters able to take the initiative in finding jobs as pastoral associates, chaplains, social workers, and so forth, but they could also seek these in parishes and institutions not traditionally associated with their community.

Prior to Vatican II, there were strong bonds between religious communities and the parish schools where they served. It would be very unusual to have sisters from multiple communities working in the same parish. Because of this relationship, a particular parish felt a close connection with particular orders. After Vatican II, however, it was not unusual for parishes to hire members of various communities to meet the desire to have religious sisters working at the parish school or on the parish staff. In some cases, a parish hired sisters from various communities because the community that was traditionally identified with the parish could no longer supply any new sisters due to the diminishment of their order.

Three important dynamics accounted for diminishing numbers in the communities:

1. Loss of members through death
2. Sisters leaving religious life
3. Fewer young women entering religious life

The net result was that the workforce was diminishing at a higher rate than it was being replenished. Therefore it became apparent that the congregations would no longer be able to supply the workforce of sisters that people had grown to know and take for granted. These dynamics impacted the hypothetical school of St. Philip's. Perhaps the observations of John Fialka in *Sisters: Catholic Nuns and the Making of America* are helpful:

While the internal debates and the voting over how to comply with the true spirit of Vatican II went on and on, the numbers of young women wanting to enter convents suddenly dropped to record lows. Within the ranks of the Mercies, by 1971 nearly one out of six sisters had voted against religious life with her feet. It was much the same in other orders and this was just the beginning of the exodus. The great, selfless machine that had spread hope, shaped young minds, and nursed sufferers for generations in America had begun to falter. It had survived wars, plagues, frontier life, numbing poverty and mindless bigotry, but something about the tumultuous 1960s was beginning to destroy it.[6]

To return to our hypothetical example, Sister Anne, the principal, was now entering her tenth year, far beyond the typical tenure of sister principals. However, in 1974, her community adopted the open-placement model. Sister Anne liked the people of the parish, had relatives nearby, and found it a good fit. She also enjoyed the company of two sisters who entered as classmates and who chose to work at St. Philip's at the beginning of the 1976–1977 school year, Sister Maria and Sister Rita.

In 1979 Sister Maria was told by her doctor that she could no longer teach full-time, so she worked in the Learning Resource Center during the afternoons four days a week. In 1979 Sister Rita needed to move to an assignment closer to her aging father, who needed some extra help, so by the end of this school year, Sister Anne remained as principal and Sister Maria was working part-time.

The pastor was concerned that the convent, which was built for ten sisters and now had two people rattling around in it, was not the best use of the space or the best living situation for the sisters; the sisters also felt the burden of maintaining such a large house. He suggested that they move to a nearby apartment complex so that the building could be utilized as a day care center, so this was done.

At the end of 1980, Sister Maria's health needed closer monitoring, and the commute from the apartment to the school was becoming a challenge, so she took a part-time job at the motherhouse, leaving Sister Anne as the last member of her community. She had arrived in the parish in 1965 as the eighth-grade teacher, then in 1967 acquired the additional job of principal. Her goal was to remain as principal for five more years.

During this time (1965–1985), the parish had grown and had hired other sisters from various communities to work as pastoral associates for the catechumenate, religious educators, ministers to the elderly, and social workers. For this reason, Sister Anne's community was not as strongly identified with the parish as it had been.

Upon Sister Anne's retirement in 1985, there was an enormous reception thanking her and the community for their years of service. She was able to educate the children of some of her former students. Sister Anne planned to work as a tutor to women getting their GEDs at a shelter sponsored by her community, while living at the motherhouse. Sister Anne's departure concluded the presence and ministry of her community's service to St. Philip's. The people of the parish always maintained communication with the sisters through various venues. The period of the sisters' strong identity and presence at St. Philip's had slowly, almost imperceptibly, diminished. Now it would be a fond and cherished memory.

Though fictional and positive, this scenario unfolded in countless parishes across the United States. Table 6.1 and figure 6.1 give a clearer understanding of the transition that so many parish schools experienced. However, there are some nuances from this model worth considering that are drawn from the experiences of the sisters who were the last members of their communities to serve in a school. Sometimes the school simply closed due to the small number of students and the extraordinary financial burden to operate such a school; this kind of closing is not the focus or interest of this book. Instead, the focus is on the experiences of the sisters who were the final community members at schools that continued to operate.

Time to Say Farewell

Many sisters found themselves in the situation of Sister Anne, who was described in the preceding hypothetical model. That is, after the congregation's shift to open placement for choosing assignments, a single sister or small band of two or three realized that there would be no sisters to follow them. The relationship of a community with a parish and its school was typically a bond that lasted for many years and most likely was taken for granted. No one could have foreseen the post–Vatican II demographics of religious life and its impact on Catholic schools.

If there had been some inkling of the impending diminishment of sisters, probably each parish would have believed that its school was special and would be spared the coming exodus. Most parishioners thought the sisters would be around to serve as educators in perpetuity.

From these parishes many young women had entered the communities serving the school, which meant the sisters were the daughters and friends of parishioners. The parish, along with Catholic schools, provided the primary pipelines to the novitiate from the family home. *Your parish* was Catholic

Table 6.1. Hypothetical Diminishment of Sisters at St. Philip School

School Year	Number of Sisters	Number of Lay Teachers
1985–2000	0	10
1980–1985	1	9
1979–1980	2	9
1978–1979	2	8
1977–1978	3	7
1976–1977	3	7
1975–1976	1	9
1974–1975	1	9
1973–1974	2	8
1972–1973	3	7
1971–1972	3	7
1970–1971	4	6
1969–1970	6	4
1968–1969	6	4
1967–1968	7	3
1966–1967	7	2
1965–1966	7	2

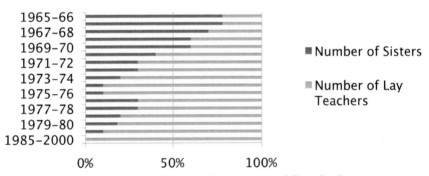

Figure 6.1. Hypothetical Diminishment of Sisters at St. Philip School

shorthand for ethnicity, socioeconomic status, the priests you knew, and which order of sisters shaped your education and success.

Those sisters who were the last members of their communities to serve in elementary schools exited the schools either under the open-placement policy or at the direction of the community's leadership according to protocols that were adopted. It would be difficult to calculate which scenario of departure would be more difficult for these individual sisters. Each model presented difficulties for the sisters on the front line.

If a group of sisters were the last members under the open-placement policy, they often felt a personal responsibility to prop up the community's presence and commitment to a parish and might make a case with the community's leadership to give special consideration to a particular place by trying to encourage someone to come to the parish. However, this solicitude and determination would simply be unmanageable and impossible with the diminishing numbers of sisters entering and fewer sisters interested in the educational apostolate. Advanced aging and declining health sometimes necessitated a withdrawal, and parishioners could easily understand this scenario.

However, a parish in which sisters were withdrawn according to criteria set by the religious community might experience varying degrees of confusion and anger. This was especially true when parish families saw three or four healthy and effective educators suddenly reassigned to other schools. The history of every religious community will show the opening, closing, or withdrawal from various apostolates. The list of ministerial works a community has sponsored over its history is impressive. Indeed, it would probably be more of an exception than a rule to still be in *all* the schools or projects that the community originally adopted. The ministries of the Sisters of St. Louis are illustrative of this phenomenon (see table 6.2).

Some sisters also chose to move to other schools that they felt were more in harmony with the direction and needs of their community's renewal, especially in responding to serving the poor. Not infrequently, sisters stated that they wanted to work in schools that were underresourced more than the typical middle-class Catholic school.

Table 6.2. The Ministries of the Sisters of St. Louis

Institution	City/Arch/Diocese	Begun	Withdrew
Nativity Elementary	Los Angeles	1949	
St. Cyprian	Los Angeles	1950	
Corpus Christi	Los Angeles	1951	
St. Bede	Los Angeles	1952	1987
Our Lady Help of Christians	Los Angeles	1953	1962
St. Anthony Claret	Orange	1957	1994
Our Lady of Refuge	Los Angeles	1953	1977
Our Lady of Malibu	Los Angeles	1958	2005
Holy Name of Mary	Los Angeles	1957	2007
St. Louis of France	Los Angeles	1956	2007
St. Mel	Los Angeles	1958	2006
Cathedral Chapel	Los Angeles	1968	1987
Blessed Sacrament	Orange	1979	1990
St. Joseph	Los Angeles	1956	1997
St. Robert	Sacramento	1957	1975
San Miguel	Los Angeles	1987	1990
Christ the King	Los Angeles	1982	1988
Our Lady of Grace	Los Angeles	1985	1995
St. Anselm	Los Angeles	1988	2003
St. Dorothy	Los Angeles	1990	2004
St. Anne	Los Angeles	1997	1999
St. Finbar	Los Angeles	2000	2003
St. Louise de Marillac	Los Angeles	1991	2004
St. Joseph	Alameda	2002	
Beatitudes of Our Lord	Los Angeles	1991	1999
St. Odilia	Los Angeles	1990	1992
Mother of Sorrows	Los Angeles	1994	1995
St. Pancratius	Los Angeles	1998	2000
Immaculate Conception	Los Angeles	1990	1992
Immaculate Conception	San Bernardino	1977	1983
St. Bridget	San Francisco	1980	1981
Holy Angels	Los Angeles	1989	1991
Louisville Kdgt.	Los Angeles	1958	1982
Mater Dei High School	Orange	1952	
Bishop Amat	Los Angeles	1957	
Louisville High School	Los Angeles	1959	
St. Anthony High School	Los Angeles	1974	1976
		1979	1980
Bellarmine Jefferson High School	Los Angeles	1993	2000
Chaminade High School	Los Angeles	1994	2005
St. Pius X High School	Los Angeles	1980	1985
St. Genevieve High School	Los Angeles	1976	1977
		1986	1993

(continued)

Table 6.2. (*continued*)

Institution	City/Arch/Diocese	Begun	Withdrew
Santa Margarita High School	Orange	1993	1994
Lanterman Dev. Center	Pomona	1985	
Home Missions	Ahoskie, NC	1992	
Queen of Angels Jr. Seminary	Los Angeles	1977	1980
St. John Seminary	Los Angeles	1967	2003
St. Meinrad School of Theology	Indiana, IN	1980	1984
		1990	1994
Catholic University of America	Washington, DC	1992	1997
Loyola Marymount University	Los Angeles	1983	
Mt. St. Mary's College	Los Angeles	1984	1990
Washington Theological Union	Washington, DC	1997	2004
Holy Trinity Parish Adult Education	Los Angeles	1978	2002
St. Jude Parish Adult Education	Los Angeles	1997	2003
St. Bernadine Parish Adult Education	Los Angeles	1997	2001
St. Pashal Baylon Adult Education	Los Angeles	1981	1983
Our Lady of the Valley	Los Angeles	1988	1993
Mission Santa Barbara	Los Angeles	1987	1988
Dept. of Catholic Schools	Los Angeles	1965	2007
Dept. of Religious Education	Los Angeles	1980	1981
Office of Diocesan Spirituality	Los Angeles	1984	
Dept. of Catholic Schools	Orange	1977	1991
Center of Spiritual Development	Orange	2001	
Dept. of Catholic Schools	San Diego	2000	
University of San Diego	San Diego	2001	
ASCA	San Diego	2001	
Office for Catechesis	Chicago	1999	
Office of Diocesan Spirituality	Salt Lake City	1996	2006
Soledad Enrichment Center	Los Angeles	1984	1986
LAMP Adult Center	Los Angeles	1995	1998
Community Adult Ed.	Los Angeles	1996	1998
A.F. International School	Los Angeles	2001	2003
U.N. Center for Better World	New York	1980	1985
District Dept. Public Schools	Long Beach	1990	1997

CHAPTER SEVEN

∾

The Sisters Reflect
upon Their Experiences

Michael Fullan, professor emeritus at the Ontario Institute for Studies in Education at the University of Toronto and an international authority on organizational change, has written extensively on the process of change and how it impacts people; perhaps even more familiar is the work of Dr. Elisabeth Kübler-Ross and her stages of grief (denial, anger, bargaining, depression, and acceptance). While many of the sisters who were the last members of their communities to serve in a school were agents of change and transition, on another level they had to process their own grief. The change was neither mechanical nor abstract, but it was very personal; this experience is rarely told or recounted in the stories of Catholic schools. Consider the multiple emotions and realities that each sister carried, whether she was a principal or teacher.

First and foremost, each sister was an ambassador of her religious community and needed to represent the concerns and needs of the congregation. She was also invested in the community and the parish school. More often than not, leading a Catholic school meant managing innumerable financial headaches, over which a person might have had little control.

These sisters were human beings whose emotional ties to the schools they served were strong. Their responsibility to implement the community's withdrawal from a parish may not have been entirely one with which they agreed, and this was never easy. The responses to withdrawal were different, in part because sometimes the trigger was a corporate decision of the community; in other cases, withdrawal was the end result of an open-placement system.

Sister Margaret Mary Stoverink, ASCJ, and Sister Kathleen Mary Coonan, ASCJ, share a good laugh with their students at St. Raphael School in Bridgeport, Connecticut.

When Community Leaders Decide to Withdraw

No community could be happy about the prospect of withdrawing from a parish school. Communities of sisters esteemed their relationships with parishioners. Recognizing the aging of the community, the fact that fewer women were entering, and the loss of sisters who left religious life, it was clear that congregations faced very painful and difficult decisions about the distribution of their most important resource: personnel.

It was apparent that a downward trend was unfolding and communities could not supply the number of sisters that each parish desired. Like the hypothetical situation of Sister Anne at St. Philip's school, attrition was indeed creeping into each school. Nevertheless, provincials and their team of advisors or councilors needed to develop a strategic plan that would help them to deal objectively with the diminishing numbers.

Such strategic planning often engaged the membership of a community in various chapter meetings or other forms of dialogue; these discussions might take place within individual convents or apostolates, or in regional meetings. As the wisdom of a community was clarified, after much discussion and prayer, a plan would be put in place. One criterion for deciding to withdraw may have been the viability of a school. Sometimes economic realities and social changes would dictate that a school might have to consolidate with another school or close. When many families with school-aged children moved out of neighborhoods, parishes no longer needed a school, or the parish could no longer sustain a school for so few children. In such cases, parishes often would consolidate schools into a single regional school, after considering both prospective students and the state of the facilities. Such transitions are often harbingers of bad news for a neighborhood or parish.

Economic Factors

On January 28, 2008, in his final State of the Union address, President George W. Bush expressed his concern about the number of faith-based schools closing in urban cores of major cities. He called a summit to address the causes and to suggest strategies to alter this trend. Bush remarked,

> We must also do more to help children when their schools do not measure up. Thanks to the D.C. Opportunity Scholarships you approved, more than 2,600 of the poorest children in our nation's capital have found new hope at a faith-based or other non-public school. Sadly, these schools are disappearing at an alarming rate in many of America's inner cities. So I will convene a White House summit aimed at strengthening these lifelines of learning. And to open the doors of these schools to more children, I ask you to support a new $300 million program called Pell Grants for Kids. We have seen how Pell Grants help low-income college students realize their full potential. Together, we've expanded the size and reach of these grants. Now let us apply that same spirit to help liberate poor children trapped in failing public schools.[1]

Bush's concern included Catholic schools, which account for the vast majority of these vulnerable schools. Most politicians and elected leaders realize that Catholic schools provide incalculable benefits to neighborhoods and cities. In many ways, their closure and consolidation serves as the metaphorical *canary in the mineshaft* regarding the health of a neighborhood. If a neighborhood is prospering, families will readily seek to live in that area and be drawn to it for its safety, quality of its schools, shopping, and various other amenities. A vibrant parish life will also entice people to settle in a particular region.

In some neighborhoods where Catholic schools are flourishing and have waiting lists, realtors are constantly badgering pastors to expand their schools to accommodate families who want a Catholic education for their children. In neighborhoods riddled with crime, poverty, and other social ills, a Catholic school can serve as a beacon of hope and stability but only for so long. When all of the studies and analyses have been conducted about the future of a school, it is ultimately finances and a lack of resources that cause a closure.

Many middle-class families and those aspiring to better their lives might desire to have their children in a Catholic school, but their inability to meet the rising cost of tuition leaves them with little choice but to withdraw their children and send them to public schools or to increasingly popular charter schools. Frequently enough, the Catholic elementary school's health most likely reflects the stability of the parish and, *de facto*, the larger neighborhood.

Parish leaders of the past and present have been challenged to assess the growth or decline of their neighborhoods and congregations. To the degree that a parish is financially solvent and vibrant, it will be able to subsidize a school to a great extent, especially with the help of fundraising events and tuition. However, if families are moving out of a neighborhood, the collection basket's contents will follow those families.

In cases where schools were consolidated because of these economic factors, it is doubtful that there was any expectation that sisters would continue to staff a school, especially if the school building that closed was one where a particular group of sisters worked. The choice to keep a particular campus open likely came with a presumption that the sisters at that school would continue to minister there. Recall that in this era it would be a rare parish without a convent for the teaching sisters. Hence, the sisters of that particular parish would simply continue living in their home.

The sisters at the other schools would have to negotiate transportation, new traditions, and ways of operating a school. Despite good intentions and a desire to make a new venture work, two different communities with differing educational philosophies collaborating in one school simply would not work for long. Consequently, those sisters staffing schools slated for consolidation at another campus had an opportunity to exit with a bit less turmoil.

Schools rarely begin a discussion of reconfiguration when they are strong or when there is an opportunity for growth and improvement by working together. This dynamic is nowhere truer than in Catholic schools that consolidate. Of course, there is obligatory rhetoric about how this merger is going to enhance the learning opportunities of the students and invigorate an even stronger school that will materialize from the otherwise struggling institutions.

Families, pastors, and educational leaders will muster all the possible energy and enthusiasm for the success of the project, but in the end, when a school closes, it is a tragic day for the parish, neighborhood, and community.

The parish that may lose the school campus will often treat the new institution like a stepchild, and the pastor at such a parish may breathe a sigh of relief to be unburdened by the day-to-day operation of the school.

The sisters at a school that faced such a consolidation might continue to staff it, but typically, the sisters who had been at the campus that closed were generally reassigned to other apostolates or missions of that order. If both schools had been sponsored by one community of sisters, then the prospect for a genuine consolidation would be enhanced.

Those lay teachers who were teaching at a school that closed might have access to joining the new faculty, but one can see where a limited number of positions might present a human resource nightmare. It is reasonable to imagine that sisters who could count on job security, and were more mobile, could easily elect to forfeit a teaching position for a layperson, given that a layperson's roots and family might make working in another part of the city or state difficult. Given the paltry salaries and benefits, lay teachers had little incentive for such moves.

How One Community Withdrew

Over time religious congregations have continually faced changing realities and demographics that elicited corporate adaptation. This adaptation and change, growth and diminishment, is part of the natural ebb and flow of the history of religious life. The Trinitarian Fathers and Brothers, for instance, were founded in the twelfth century to serve as personal ransoms or exchanges for captured crusaders. The community eventually had to adapt to changing times, or acknowledge that their purpose had been served and stop accepting candidates. They chose to broaden their mission.

Communities of sisters have also had to consider their changing world, and this has been a continual process, something that is dynamic and dialogical with the world. At the same time, they have tried to preserve what is essential in their rule.

Sisters completing an assignment at a consolidated school were most likely reassigned to other ministries of the order, or a new apostolate was adopted.

Sisters were often directed by superiors to break the news of a decision to the people; the sister who was announcing the community's withdrawal may have had conflicting feelings about the decision. "Sister Therese" recalls the following scene withdrawing from a parish school in 1987:

Our regional community had given the then leadership team of three sisters almost a mandate to begin withdrawing from some of the many elementary schools we staffed—both because of fewer incoming vocations and a chapter call to respond in some new ways to the needs of the poor. St. Barbara's was the first school chosen because it met several of the criteria they had deemed appropriate:

- The school itself needed to be strong and thriving.
- The faculty needed to be good and somewhat stable.
- The parish needed to be able to afford a lay principal's salary.
- There had to be potential lay leadership already in evidence.

After serious deliberation, the regional superior wrote a letter to the school staff, the parish council, and the school parent community at large. They scheduled meetings with all three groups on the same day! The faculty took it the hardest; one key person described the experience as painful, as "having been served divorce papers."

Their great anger and hurt was a result of their loyalty to and love for us. They also knew I had left St. Barbara's as principal two years earlier to take on a new school in the [archdiocese] and the Sister who replaced me was only willing to "hold the fort" for a year or two. One member of the parish council, a judge, recognizing that our regional superior was near tears as she gave them notice of our upcoming withdrawal from the school and parish convent, gently told her, "You do not have to carry our pain as well as your own."

Then at a *standing room only* PTO general meeting the superior once again contextualized the need for us to withdraw from some of our strongest schools. Several parents expressed sadness with deep appreciation for our community's presence in the school and parish since the early 1950s. Another owned that they as parents hadn't done much to foster religious vocations among their own children and understood the decreasing numbers in our order. (emphasis in original)

Like so many of the reports of withdrawals, this account describes the real sadness and grief that followed an announcement of departure from a parish. The regret was apparent on the part of the parish community as well as the sisters. Because the sisters always had assignments awaiting them, it might have seemed that they simply picked up their few belongings and marched off to a new school with little or no remorse, perhaps only revealing their hearts to their closest friends or other community members. But there is abundant evidence that the sisters experienced a very painful transition.

One of the most singular comments in "Sister Therese's" account, not reported by any others, was the recognition among the parents that they had not done much to encourage religious vocations. In 1965, when the number of sisters reached an all-time high with 178,954, Catholics were routinely encouraging their children to consider religious life or the priesthood. But during the tumultuous years that followed, attitudes began to shift.[2]

Attitudes toward Religious Vocations

There had been a time when a Catholic family was quite receptive to having a daughter in religious life or a son in the priesthood, but that was in the days of large families who were steeped in Catholic culture. Catholic families began to shrink during the last decades of the twentieth century and there was a dramatic shift in Mass attendance, parish involvement, and Catholic reading.[3] These changes were contemporaneous with the large departures of women religious from the schools and a drop in vocations to religious life and the priesthood. All of these factors contributed to an attitude that pursuing a religious vocation might be a difficult life choice instead of a stable, joyful vocation.

During at least three quarters of the twentieth century, Catholic children were regularly encouraged to ponder the possibility that God might be calling them to be a co-worker as a priest or religious sister or brother. Vocation talks were routinely given by the priests of the parish or by priests and brothers of visiting missionary orders, and Catholic-centric textbooks and readers were rich with stories of saints who answered the call to religious life. Naturally, the close association of the sisters of the parish with their students also provided innumerable opportunities for informal inquiries, as well as official presentations on religious life. It would have been unfathomable to imagine a day without some level of vocational promotion, whether subliminal or overt.

Although researchers agree that the large number of vocations in the past century were an unprecedented historical blip on the demographic screen, the desire for religious sisters, brothers, and priests to staff the schools did not decrease along with the numbers. Even today in those elementary and secondary schools where religious continue to maintain a presence, parents will often inquire about the number of religious working at the school. A greater number of sisters, brothers, and priests will often correlate with a positive attitude toward the school and elicit a sense of pride.

Many of the orders of sisters who continue to receive good numbers of aspirants into their novitiates and communities and are still committed to the educational apostolate in a meaningful way experience a great demand for their sisters. One provincial, "Sister Monique," commented on the small but steady number of applicants to her order. She noted that the community did all it could to renew itself in the spirit and letter of Vatican II. Their sisters were generous in their willingness to serve the Church and to be counted upon to serve the needs of the institutions of the dioceses where they worked. But she noted the demands are great: "We're doing everything we can, but if God wants us to continue, He must supply the sisters."

The types of communities and religious vocations that are currently attracting new members can be tracked, described, and analyzed, but ultimately it is the work of the Holy Spirit in cooperation with discerning persons that will yield a vocation. A supportive environment in the family home and parish will help a vocation grow by listening to the Holy Spirit. But the families of St. Barbara's Parish, as described by "Sister Therese," acknowledged that they had done very little to encourage young women to consider religious life beyond the fact that people appreciated the ministry of the sisters at the parish. Unfortunately, they expected a steady supply of sisters from somewhere else and never dreamed of a day when their parish would not be among the priority assignments for the order.

Sister Boniface, the former superior of a community that receives a large number of applicants and novices each year but still can't keep up with the demand from parishes and schools requesting their sisters' services, notes that in her reply to these requests, she typically included the following admonition: "When you send us the girls, we'll send you the nuns."

Many people have vague notions of vocations and their origins. Some parishes had an expectation akin to entitlement to the ministry of the teaching sisters. There was often a disengaged attitude that assumed God would provide the ongoing presence of sisters drawn from families other than one's own.

When the supply could no longer meet all the demands of the parish community, the sisters would need to withdraw from the parish. At that point, any discussion of doing more to promote and encourage vocations to the religious life, while it is an ongoing need, was certainly too late to alter the course of leaving a particular school.

Breaking the News to the Parish

Sister Mary Peter Traviss, OP, who served as the education supervisor for the Dominican Sisters of Mission San José for twenty-four years, notes that it was often the duty of the education supervisor to deliver the news of the religious community's withdrawal from a parish. The news was never welcome and often created a backlash of ill feelings between the sisters and the parish. Sister Mary Peter recalls delivering the news of withdrawal to one parish in rural California where her community had served: "If they would have had stones, they would have thrown them at me."

Often parishes tried to negotiate a bargain with the community to maintain some of the sisters in the school. Frequently, the parish would object and claim "if only we had known you were thinking of withdrawing, we could have done some things differently." At this point in a school's history, the economics and demographics of a parish may have been in rapid change or decline.

But sometimes the departure of the sisters did not spell imminent disaster or closure for a school. In fact, sometimes communities withdrew precisely because the school was quite viable, and the community felt its investment could be better utilized in parish schools struggling to survive.

Every apostolic mission has a purpose and set of goals; sometimes these are ongoing and will only be completed when the *parousia* arrives. However, religious congregations who set out to help poor European immigrants many years later found that the grandchildren and great-grandchildren of those immigrants were no longer in need. They had found their place in society. So, like the Trinitarians who were mentioned earlier, a religious community frequently assesses its ministries to determine if they are still meeting the vision of the order.

Many communities began to ask questions about serving in affluent parish schools when so many schools in underresourced parishes were struggling. It is not an easy question to resolve because of numerous issues. As Sister Mary Peter recalls, "Some parish communities felt they were being punished for being successful when the sisters were withdrawn."

She noted a conundrum from a successful Cristo Rey High School: "A young man was not admitted [to a particular program] because his father made more money than the limit specified for enrollment. The father had to work two jobs for his family; he complained that he was being punished for working extremely hard." It is a reality that economic class sometimes drives ministerial choices, especially when communities already bound to poverty choose to make a preferential option for the poor.

Religious will always feel the need to seek the poor Christ when decisions are to be made. One of the Ignatian values from which many apostolic communities draw insight is that of holy indifference—that is, an attitude or disposition flowing from the First Principle and Foundation set out by St. Ignatius Loyola in his *Spiritual Exercises*:

- The human person is created to praise, reverence, and serve God Our Lord, and by doing so, to save his or her soul.
- All other things on the face of the earth are created for human beings in order to help them pursue the end for which they are created.

- It follows from this that one must use other created things, in so far as they help towards one's end, and free oneself from them, in so far as they are obstacles to one's end.
- To do this, we need to make ourselves indifferent to all created things, provided the matter is subject to our free choice and there is no other prohibition.
- Thus, as far as we are concerned, we should not want health more than illness, wealth more than poverty, fame more than disgrace, a long life more than a short one, and similarly for all the rest, but we should desire and choose only what helps us more towards the end for which we are created.[4]

Clearly, the wealthy also have souls and needs to be served, and many religious generously labor in affluent parishes and institutions. However, during the process of renewal, many religious communities re-embraced their founding mission to serve those in greatest need. Thus, when it came time for making ministerial decisions, these communities realized that certain schools would continue to flourish without their presence, while other schools were in greater need of their services. Urgency of need helped the leadership teams to rank ministerial priorities.

"Sister Sara Mary," whose community had been associated with a parish for nearly seventy years, describes the withdrawal from a school with this narrative:

Our sisters staffed the school and parish until 2001. At the time of our departure we had five sisters at "St. Veronica's": principal of the school (me), one full-time middle school teacher, one full-time coordinator of religious education (the religious education program had over 500 students) who also taught a few classes in the school, one part-time development director, and one part-time pastoral minister who also worked part-time at a Catholic hospital.

When I was asked by my community to move to another area of the country to open the first-ever Catholic high school in that city, I learned for the first time that I would not be replaced with a member of my community in the principal position. This was in January of 2001. Within the next month I was to learn that the sisters would no longer be in the school, but possibly might stay in the parish.

By the end of February our provincial superior came to our house to tell us that our sisters would no longer be serving at St. Veronica's once the academic year finished. Our pastor found out the next day. In March we drafted a letter to the school parents and parents of students in religious education.

At the same time when the letter was mailed, we met with our faculties (school and religious education program) to tell them of our withdrawal from the parish. It was difficult to share this news with them, as we had been in the parish for sixty-four years.

With regard to the school, the faculty members were worried about who the next principal would be and what it would mean for the school. The lay principal who was hired turned out to be a local Catholic who retired that year from the public school system and wasn't worried about his salary since his retirement plan was so good.

He used money from his salary to purchase things for the school that we could not afford up to that point, since we bought only absolute necessities. (We were trying to make budget each year.) He is a fine educator and was very excited to begin his years as a Catholic school principal. There couldn't have been a better person picked for this time of transition.

"Sister Maya" from this same community, who had formerly served at this school, describes the plummeting enrollment and how few young families were moving into this Rust Belt city. Though she had previously taught at the school, she was now a pastoral associate, a role she enjoyed since she knew the parish community quite well.

She described the shock in the community of not having even a year's notice to prepare people. Sister Maya described one man who could not face the empty church pew where the sisters traditionally worshipped. Their absence was a sacred, if sad, reminder of the many women who had lovingly served over the years.

This sister also noted an unfortunate perception that many people had about the transition. Sister Maya described a mistaken understanding that the pastor did not treat the sisters well and because of this callous treatment, the sisters decided to leave the parish. In fact, the pastor had been proactive in improving the convent. Though the sisters were on a lower pay scale and even took less than the designated religious pay scale, there was no validity to the assertion that the pastor's mistreatment of the sisters was the reason for withdrawal. The sisters and the pastor were on good terms.

Yet another sister who served in this apostolate, "Sister Mary James," was the community's superior and had further reflections. Upon her arrival several years before the departure of the sisters, a different pastor, who was an alcoholic, had been at the parish. Sister Mary James described herself as a leader who was able to deal with difficult pastors, and this complex situation was resolved speedily, because the pastor was sent for treatment.

She described the convent as dark and drafty, but the new pastor ushered in a season of change for the better. At the time there were eight sisters working in the school. The new pastor met with the principal and asked her to consult with the sisters and to make a prioritized list of the school and convent. Within three years the entire complex had been revamped.

She praised this priest's community-building skills, related not only to bricks and mortar but also, and more importantly, to building and deepening the spirituality of the community. He would often join the sisters for meals and gave full confidence to Sister Mary James, which enabled her to share her gifts with others. She noted that parishioners took ownership for the parish and its activities; it was a place full of vibrant energy and people working closely together. Even though the sisters no longer serve there, she noted that it continues to be a vibrant parish.

The sisters who were at this school at the time of its closure have slightly varying views of the departure, but what was evident with each of them was their deep love for the people of the parish. They also spoke of the legacy and sacrifice of several generations of their sisters. The separation and loss that each sister experienced affected each one's spirits. As Sister Mary James commented, "that accumulation of seventy-three years of service was something deep in our hearts."

Here are the guidelines the community used for assessing their missions.

Some criteria for withdrawing from a place of ministry:

1. Continued lack of support and cooperation impedes the ministry.
2. We can no longer meet the needs of the ministry.
3. The responsibilities of the ministries can be assumed by others.
4. We cannot assure the continued staffing of the ministry due to diminishing personnel.
5. Our continued presence is impacted by factors beyond our control.
6. The circumstances of the ministry are not conducive to community life.
7. The original intent for ministering in that mission is now completed.
8. Our financial investment is contrary to good stewardship.

These eight points offer a prudent and balanced set of criteria to determine apostolic effectiveness. They are flexible enough to apply to a wide range of situations. Note the balance of interests and needs of both the community as well as the apostolate. These criteria were no doubt crafted out of many painful situations with an attempt to objectify standards as well as possible so that good decisions might transcend politics, personalities, and undue influences to the greatest extent possible. But when all is said and done, the lonely and difficult work of a provincial is to implement the decision. Even though a leadership team may have made the decision, one person usually bears the heat of answering questions and listening to all stakeholders.

From the perspective of a parish that is receiving the sad news of losing its sisters, the pastor and people would have wanted to review each of the points on the list and then make a strong case for the sisters' continued presence and ministry, similar to the way parishioners try to make a case to a bishop on why their parish shouldn't close.

This anywhere-but-here dynamic recalls a story about the controversial John Cardinal Cody that may be apocryphal, but, as the Italians say, *se non è vero, è ben trovato* ("even if it's not true, it makes a good story").

Before going to Chicago in the mid-1960s, Cody, then the archbishop of New Orleans, was listening to some people making a case on behalf of a struggling parish slated for closing due to rezoning that was causing people to move out as light industry moved in. The longtime parishioners who were not moving were making a case for the importance that the parish had played in their lives and how their future as a parish, even if diminished, must be a top priority of the diocese. Cody remarked, so legend has it, "The salvation of just one soul is indeed enough justification for the existence of a parish. However, I would not want to be pastor of that parish." The parish was dissolved and reabsorbed by neighboring parishes.

This NIMBYism (Not in My Backyard) was especially present in parish schools where the sisters withdrew. Sometimes the transitions of sisters leaving were rancorous among the sisters and their leadership. Sometimes there was tension between the people of the parish and the community of sisters. The work of renewal that followed Vatican II gave everyone a greater voice and sense of participation. The sisters, as well as the laity, were more confident in forming their own opinions and expressing their views. A new sense of participating in ecclesial life had begun, one that valued participation. It was not always an egalitarian or democratic sense of participation, but one that sought informed contributions on appropriate matters. In some cases, because of such open communication, the transition of sisters out of the parish was fairly peaceful.

Peaceful Transitions

More tranquil transitions took place where lay leaders, cognizant of their baptismal gifts to spread the Good News, had accepted a new paradigm that did not exclusively restrict ministry to the work of priests and sisters. These lay leaders saw that they had a contribution to make, not only in their families but also in the workplace and in their parish communities.

When parishioners had an initial and ongoing catechetical experience that was solid and authentic, they were better prepared to face a changing world and church. They had become active members instead of passive observers. One Midwestern parish, St. Gertrude's Parish, is an example of this model that was becoming prevalent across the United States.

This parish had prepared its people spiritually and catechetically in such a way that no matter what transitions were unfolding, their attitudes and dispositions were anchored in God and their faith, and not the personalities or structures that were changing. Therefore, when the sisters serving their parish, the Sisters of St. Joseph of Carondelet (CSJ), planned to reduce their teaching and administrative staff in a two-year withdrawal during the 1970s, the parish families were able to make the transition with grace and renewed commitment to the educational enterprise of their elementary school.

Following prescribed criteria, the sisters chose to withdraw from this particular school that had been staffed for nearly seventy years by the same congregation of sisters. The parish was considered affluent but comprised a diversity of members from several socioeconomic groups. The school had always been strong and its future was bright; the parish had also been a home to many religious vocations, not only to this specific congregation but also to other orders of sisters, as well as diocesan and religious orders of priests. When the sisters realized that they could no longer meet all of their institutional commitments, they planned to depart this thriving parish.

The sisters were known and loved by the people for many generations. The close work and preparation for the transition was carefully announced two years prior to the actual farewell, so there was time for planning the future. The pastor, the principal, faculty, and the leadership of the motherhouse were clear and optimistic about the transition; this had always been a strong school and the people were committed to continuing its development.

There was also a clear understanding that other schools in the diocese that were being served by these sisters, and would continue to have them, were not in the same financial situation to continue without the sisters and their low salaries.

Hence, the parish recognized its good fortune in its ability to sustain an elementary school without the presence of women religious, and they generously recognized that another Catholic school would be sustained because of the redistribution of the sisters. This attitude among the people developed through the parish-wide catechesis that followed Vatican II.

Under the leadership of the pastors during and after the years of Vatican II, the parish sought to engage the documents of the Council with a special emphasis on the laity taking leadership in the parish. This ambitious program had organized the parish into smaller neighborhood clusters where people would meet and discuss matters of the church. In many ways, these parish efforts were preparing people to assume responsibilities that had always been the exclusive purview of the clergy and religious.

By wisely and responsibly interpreting the vision of Vatican II, the parish was prepared for the sisters' decision to leave the school. Naturally, there was sadness and regret, but people had been prepared to realize that very few things were written in stone. Being able to face the future with such confidence and optimism exemplified the insight on change that John Henry Cardinal Newman (1801–1890) once offered in *An Essay on the Development of Christian Doctrine*: "In a higher world it is otherwise, but here below to live is to change, and to be perfect is to have changed often."[5]

CHAPTER EIGHT

~

When a School Closed

One of the sadder experiences a parish may face is the closure of its school with no option for consolidation. More often than not, these schools were constructed at a tremendous financial sacrifice of many working-class people who were determined to provide a Catholic education for their own children and for the generations to come. Usually a large portion of the parish budget was spent on its school, and several generations would be socialized into the life of the parish community through its school. But when the demographics no longer provided viable numbers to operate an increasingly expensive educational enterprise, the school would close.

Sister Christian Price, ASCJ, described her experience as a principal whose nine-year tenure at St. Luke the Evangelist School in St. Louis, Missouri, included closing the school (2006–2007) after ninety-one years. Grief in all stages (denial, anger, bargaining, depression, and acceptance) operated among the people of the parish and especially among the school families.

In such situations, everyone is looking toward others for the "rules of the road" or social norms of behavior in a state of affairs that is new and stressful. A positive message was presented early on by Sister Christian and the other leaders to make the final year a good school year, and to not mentally leave the school before the formal closure.

While no group at the parish or school, such as students, parents, or alumni, would find this closing an easy task, the seventh-grade class probably took this news the hardest, since they were completing their penultimate year. They were recognized with a special certificate of promotion at the end of the year, as they would have to complete their one remaining year of elementary education at another school.

School psychologist Nan Henderson has written extensively on resiliency and the capacity of children to cope successfully with challenges and difficulties. Adults, family members, and church families all help children deal with stress and life's problems, both great and small. Starting at a new school or workplace is always a new test, but it also brings many opportunities, such as making new friends or starting with a fresh slate of social or educational expectations.

Keeping Up Appearances

The relationship between a pastor and principal is absolutely pivotal to a successful school. That point cannot be stressed enough. Presuming these are two people of goodwill with noble desires to serve the People of God, there is an abundance of common ground to build a strong, seamless community between the church and school. There is no perfect, problem-free workplace where everyone gets along and everyone is content. Nonetheless, the expansion of the Catholic school system in the United States is a testimony to the goodwill and constructive relationships between bishops, clergy, and women religious.

Deeply embedded in the Catholic culture is the Italian attitude of *la bella figura*: look good in all circumstances and present a positive face. In other words, don't air your dirty laundry in public.

This is why Catholic leaders rarely speak of problems or describe dire situations as if nothing is wrong. Catholics loathe real or perceived dissent. Hence, in a parish school where there was conflict between the pastor and school, most people would be shocked to learn of it because the principal was often trying to do damage control. Two extreme examples are worth consideration.

At a Midwestern school, "Sister Elizabeth Ann" was assigned as principal with three other members of her community. Their community had served in this school for over twenty-five years. Upon her arrival, she was aghast at the physical condition of the school, and even though she was quite accustomed to working in schools without luxuries, this school was unreasonably behind the times.

A dilapidated mimeograph machine was the most modern piece of equipment, and carbon paper was still being used to make copies. At the rectory resided a tyrant of a pastor who had no interest in the school. When he appeared at PTA meetings, he used abusive and salty language.

The provincial had sent Sister Elizabeth Ann in to see what she could do; others had evidently tried. One of her first priorities was to strengthen communication with the pastor and build a positive relationship. Meeting with the pastor was never an easy task, and she tried everything from formal appointments to invitations for coffee or meals, but he was elusive. She would go to the rectory, which she described as "the cave," to meet with him at the dining room table, hoping this relaxed environment would be conducive to communication. The parish secretary, who walked on eggshells around the man, could never offer a propitious time for a meeting.

Sister Elizabeth Ann's first project was to raise money for a new copy machine and to purchase two electric typewriters. A gym teacher had organized a marathon to raise the money to purchase these items so as not to cut into an already lean budget, but the pastor was unwilling to confer a blessing on the event. A simple ribbon-cutting duty such as this wins lots of points symbolically and builds lots of goodwill in the parish. The man was verbally abusive, dismissive, and uncivil to this principal. She needed to build goodwill among her faculty and the school families, while trying to offer respect to a man who clearly did not deserve it. It was a classic case of maintaining *la bella figura*.

There was minimal support for the convent, and one sister who became very ill had her health insurance policy canceled at a time when she needed it most. Clearly, this was not a healthy situation for these sisters despite their love for the children and parish. The religious community decided to withdraw the sisters from this apostolate.

The bishop was the first to be notified of the decision. For unknown reasons, the bishop chose to sacrifice the presence of this community of sisters in favor of this rogue pastor. The province of the sisters communicated the departure of the sisters to the pastor from their generalate in Rome.

Needless to say, the families of the parish were very sad to learn the news; they had always been extremely supportive of the sisters. The sisters arranged visits to the homes of many parishioners to share their news and bid farewell. The sisters planned a farewell Mass that took place after school ended for the year. This community would renew its vows each year on the Feast of the Sacred Heart, and this became the farewell liturgy.

The sister who had been ill also returned for the Mass. The church was packed, and it was a very emotional event, but something unexpected happened. While the sisters were kneeling in the sanctuary, they were unaware that standing behind each of them was a recent graduate of the eighth-grade class with a rose. When they stood and turned around, they were each presented with a rose by a student.

The former principal remembered the event by saying, "This gesture, more than anything, confirmed my vocation. When I turned around and saw those students, I was deeply moved." The sisters gave a candle to each teacher and a statue of the Sacred Heart as a memento. Report cards were given by the pastor, and the sisters did not go back into the convent.

Sisters at another school on the West Coast experienced similar tension with the parish clergy, which in turn contributed to the withdrawal of the sisters. "Sister Margaret" described the situation in these words:

When I arrived at "St. Leo's" there were six sisters. One teacher was part-time, the others full time, and I was a full time administrator. We maintained that number although roles changed at times. One of our sisters who taught full time in the school was also the DRE. After approximately three years, she was replaced by a sister who was a part time tutor in the school as well as the DRE.

St. Leo's School and Parish was founded by a pastor who remained pastor until approximately 1997. At that time he retired and he remained in a private dwelling serving the people of the parish until his death. The pastor did not know our community when the parish was founded. His brother met the provincial of our community a few years prior to the opening of the parish/school, was impressed by the sister he met, and passed that information onto his brother. In turn, this pastor pursued this contact until our sisters committed themselves to this mission. (Our sisters also served in various other parishes and high schools in the diocese. Currently we are no longer working in this diocese.)

The parish and school were built in the outskirts of major city proper. People thought he [the pastor] was crazy to build a parish and school in what was considered no man's land. Subdivisions grew in number and the parish served a primarily middle-class Caucasian community. By the time of our community's withdrawal in 2000 the community had changed dramatically to a Caucasian, Hispanic, Vietnamese, and Filipino community. Many of the houses in the area were repossessed by the government and another white flight began to regions further south.

We were informed that a proposal to withdraw from the school/parish was being considered in the fall of 1999. I believe the formal announcement was made by letter to school families in February of 2000. The parish was notified (through the grapevine) and formally through the parish bulletin.

Parishioners and parents of school children were devastated. They rallied to keep the sisters in their parish. They organized an S.O.S. campaign (Save Our Sisters). This was a friendly bunch but quite determined. They contacted our provincial to ask how this tide might turn. The local newspaper ran several articles on their efforts. The provincial spoke to the parents in a large gathering where she outlined basic reasons for this decision.

There was really no preparation for this transition. We did, however, have a mission statement in place that included some sense of our charism (at least the sisters were mentioned in the mission statement as founding the school with the pastor). Although parents decried this decision, they were aware of the fact that vocations were few and this impacted some of the decision to leave this parish school. (Our community is primarily on the East coast and this was an outlying area for us. At the time we left St. Leo's there were only five of us and the nearest community mission was in the Midwest.) The parents began to pray for vocations to the priesthood and religious life. (They did, however, realize that this was necessary for the future of the church, not a means of keeping their sisters at St. Leo's.)

I had a wonderful experience with the students, faculty and parents. My greatest challenge—and I believe those in leadership in the school . . . board members etc., found it an incredible challenge—was to convince the new pastor that the school was a vital part of the parish. Frankly, I believe it was the only living part of the parish.

Another sister, who worked at the parish as a teacher, offered further insights into the behavior of the new pastor, who had been the curate at this parish before being promoted to pastor. As pastor he had very little interest in the school and his distance was creating serious problems and tensions at the school. When the sisters brought their concerns to the vicar for religious, the vicar treated their apprehensions with respect and assured them that they merited action. However, the bishop told the sisters to mind their own business.

With escalating tensions, the community's decision-making council decided to withdraw from this parish's apostolates. The sisters who were actually assigned to the two schools wanted to make the announcement a year ahead of time, but the congregation's leadership decided to make the announcement and withdraw in that same school year.

"Sister Catherine" described the scene: "Our principal began delegating tasks traditionally done by the sisters, such as May crowning, special liturgies, etc. The confidence of the laity to organize these tasks was not high."

Sister Catherine recalled that "one of the hardest aspects of this time was that the sisters were all grieving and dealing with their own feelings, but we tried to minister to everyone else's grief." Anyone who has been a chief mourner at a funeral knows and feels the strain of trying to console others.

At the end there was an elegant formal dinner. There was great mutual attachment between the people and the sisters. The hospitality over the years created bonds, and sometimes the professional boundaries got blurred.

When the search began for a new principal, an experienced person was chosen. The transition months were characterized by a collaborative model with an urgency to share various projects and responsibilities that were typically done by the sisters. After the sisters had completed all their work and said all their goodbyes, the day came when they were departing for good. Another large contingent of people had assembled at the airport to give them one final blessing and to sing a song of farewell to the sisters.

This sister further reflected, "We have stayed in touch with many people through email and cards. The sense among the people was . . . that the school was not the same after the sisters left." For example, she had described First Fridays with Mass and devotions as central to the spirituality of the school and occasions on which the entire school attended. Over the years, these devotions became optional.

The sisters exercised great respect for the clergy at this parish and tried their best to follow the proper protocols for the problems that developed. Unfortunately, the dismissive tone and resistance to dealing with the problems at the parish with responsible leadership all contributed to the withdrawal of the sisters. In many ways, the choice to ignore one problem inadvertently saddled the parish with another problem that was irreversible—that of the sisters leaving.

When the leadership of a community is constantly evaluating the community's ability to meet commitments, it is far easier to withdraw from a place where their members are not heard or treated as responsible partners in ministry. One unshakable truth of religious life is job security; there is almost always a job waiting somewhere else for a competent sister, brother, or priest.

Schools Owned by the Community

Almost every community of sisters, in addition to the diocesan schools where they serve, also have their own private schools—that is, schools that are owned, operated, and staffed by the community with no outside funding. Understandably, these community-owned private schools will claim a priority.

Sisters are often prepared to teach at different grade levels or take different administrative positions. Nonetheless, the shortsighted leadership of many parishes and dioceses paved the way for communities of sisters to redistribute their members to other apostolates.

The *Catholic Sentinel*, the diocesan newspaper for the Portland diocese, described the departure of the Dominican Sisters of Mission San José from the diocese where approximately 200 sisters had served during their 119 years of service.[1] Like other orders, they cited their declining numbers and aging community as the principal reasons for the transition. There was no question of the love and respect that was mutually shared between the people and the sisters over the years.

Some of their schools and apostolates had grown, declined, and eventually closed, with the Parish of St. Therese being their sole ministry in the state. Most of their schools are in California, with five missions in Mexico. Following a two-year discernment process, they decided to withdraw from the Portland school.

The sisters also noted that this particular school was the only one of their schools where a Dominican sister was not the principal or administrator: "Leaders of the congregation have decided to focus efforts on the locations where they hold the responsibility of authority." Over the years, some sisters of the 250 member community were natives to Portland and had come to know the community by attending the schools where the sisters served. At the time of the withdrawal four sisters were living and working in the area.

Sister Gloria Marie Jones, OP, the prioress and provincial of the community, expressed her thoughts at a Mass of farewell: "Sometimes the call leads us to moments of birthing, of bringing forth new life, other times it may feel more like moments of dying, of letting go. In each moment we know our God meets us and leads us, and calls us to more—more life and always ultimately more love."[2]

When Sisters Chose to Leave under an Open-Placement System

A community decision to leave a school was deliberate; departures caused by open placement were usually a slow attrition that was much less intentional. Open placement allowed sisters to find their own assignments and have them approved by the leadership of their particular community. Frequently, sisters who were members of such communities may have been in schools where there had been an institutional agreement between the religious congregation and the parish. Many sisters continued to teach in such schools, and an ebb and flow of arrivals and departures continued, but with the inevitable diminishment of numbers.

Some sisters dreaded the day of their departures from the schools because there was a clear lack of qualified teachers or administrators to fill their shoes. It was not unheard of in Catholic schools to have faculty members with little (and, in some cases, no) formal preparation for teaching. Many simply had the gifts and skills of being good teachers. Indeed in some schools, especially in rural schools, many teachers lacked the official credentials and degrees.

"Sister Mary Jeanne" remarked, "There was a fear that mediocrity would replace the high standards we had established." In many ways the sisters constituted the teaching professionals of a school and were able to mentor and encourage their colleagues who made up in natural talent what they perhaps lacked in formal preparation. Some noted that there was a fear among many school parents, and even the sisters, that the Catholicity of the school might be diluted or compromised without the sisters. It was not unheard of for some to even wonder if you could have a Catholic school without sisters, so pervasive was their influence and presence.

"Sister Karen Marie," who had served in Catholic education for over fifty years at seventeen different schools, reflected upon her ministry and all the transitions she had seen, especially at one school where she was one of the last sisters to serve:

> There was great upset among the people of the parish, and the faculty was very divided about our departure. New ministries were opening and some of our sisters wanted to pursue these; some people understood these new needs and were supportive and others were not. At the time of our farewell, there was an overwhelming sense of loss. The school continued fairly well, but the study habits and discipline of the children were not the same.

Many observers of Catholic schools comment upon the differences they see in schools where sisters teach or had once taught. Some feel that the changes in a school without sisters, while not the end of the world, shifted the school culture. Another sister of this congregation asserted that "laity came along at an emergency time and there was not enough attention paid to the details of the transition."

Sister Mary Jeanne contrasted her experience of being the last member of her community to leave two different schools in smaller Western towns:

> In the first, we tried to prepare by looking for and hiring an excellent principal. The people feared that the sisters' departure would also minimize the school's Catholicity. Despite our search for the ideal principal, there was no response. We ended up hiring a good Catholic, but this person lacked the academic background.

Eight years later, Sister Mary Jeanne would be in a similar situation and be part of a group that was leaving a parish elementary school. This time there was better planning, utilizing the best of available resources:

> At this school we groomed lay teachers to take roles of leadership in the school. We did mentoring. Eventually, when the new principal was selected it

was someone who had not served as a principal before and who lacked experience and a degree.

This is not an isolated instance of a sister finding herself twice to be
among the last community members to withdraw from a school. However,
almost every sister interviewed expressed a profound and absolute hope to
never have to be in such circumstances again. While it was not a specific
question posed, each participant resolutely claimed it was one of the most
challenging and difficult things she had ever done, and there was rarely a
sense of satisfaction with it.

Loss of Parental Buy-In

"Sister Anita" made an interesting statement about her departure from working in schools. She noted that the parents had become so obstreperous that
she no longer wanted to work in education. She recalled that "parents didn't
want their children scolded or corrected." Such disruptive parental behavior is
the complete reversal of the Catholic school social norms of the last century,
wherein a student did not want to upset the teacher because getting in trouble
with the teacher generally meant upsetting the team of teachers and parents.

Catholic school folklore and tradition are replete with examples of the co-
hesive Catholic community. A student knew that his or her parents were on
the same team as their teachers, especially if the teacher was a sister. When
a student got into any kind of trouble with a teacher, the chief objective,
after atoning for the infraction, was to keep the said offense quiet and off
the record. For if a parent discovered that their child had upset the teacher
by doing something uncharacteristic of the family's values, which were the
same as the school's, the student would get into even more trouble at home.

Dr. Irene Oliver, professor of teacher education at Loyola Marymount
University, notes that the crazy excuses students fabricated, such as "My dog
ate my homework," were elaborate attempts to cover a crime so terrible as
missing one's homework that only an equally grand excuse, no matter how
implausible, could absolve the misdemeanor.

That parental support has significantly diminished by all accounts. The
current principal of a Los Angeles Catholic elementary school was exasper-
ated because of the chronic, widespread, and pervasive situation of children
not doing their homework. Upon expressing her concern to the school
board, the discussion zeroed in like a laser beam upon the parents: Where
were they? Each person attending the meeting then began to recount the dire
consequences awaiting anyone in their family if homework was not done.

Father Michael Garanzini, SJ, president of Loyola University Chicago and respected psychologist, has written extensively on education and family dynamics. Writing in *Catholic School Leadership: An Invitation to Lead*, he described the following familiar scenario:

> At a recent meeting of elementary and secondary school principals, the question arose: what is the most difficult aspect of your job as an administrator? Without hesitation, one veteran principal piped up: "For me, the most difficult part of the job is dealing with parents, especially parents in denial, parents who demand that their child be treated as an exception, parents with unrealistic expectations." This principal elaborated that she felt these very parents make excessive demands on her time and on the energy of her colleagues. "They just do not appreciate what we can and cannot do in the school setting." While there are numerous demands placed on educational leaders each day, there may be nothing more frustrating and time consuming than parents whose sense of entitlement can drain us emotionally and physically.[3]

Because everyone has attended school, almost everyone feels that he or she is an expert on teaching and school administration; perhaps even worse is the irresponsible behavior of some parents. Nonetheless, research does offer some explanations for the reversal of a long-held tradition of parents siding with the school's judgment in most matters. Some believe that today's parents themselves are much better educated and certainly hold degrees that are equal to, if not better than, the degrees that school leaders hold. In a former day and age, teachers usually held an academic advantage.

Another reality is that parents, overworked and overscheduled, and not always feeling they have been available to their children, may be quick to side with their children against the school's leadership.

Other important contributing cultural factors are the overall diminishment in respect for authority, which among Catholics continues to dissipate as a result of the clergy sex-abuse scandal that began receiving public attention in the 1980s. Respect and trust was squandered by the perpetrators and those who failed to correct them.

Again in *Catholic School Leadership*, Garanzini outlines the stress of modern families, but also offers some strategies for school leaders in coping with the problems these families present. However, there will be times when school leaders will reach their limit and decide that these kinds of problems demand more than they are willing to invest.

"Sister Anita," the sister who left teaching because of uncooperative parents, now works with adults. Her honesty is to be admired, and undoubtedly her reasons for leaving elementary education cannot be an isolated circumstance. The ethos and culture of Catholic schools had changed. One of the hallmarks of her community's educational philosophy was to instill respect in everyone; one would presume this applied especially toward the leadership of the school. The active participation of parents in their children's schools is encouraged and absolutely fundamental for Catholic education. If the reader does not believe that teachers and principals are under unusual pressure and unrealistic expectations from the families being served, just ask any teachers about their experience with these matters. Indeed, research has benchmarked parental involvement at Catholic schools as an indicator of social capital, a tremendous strength for a school.

> Sociology professor James S. Coleman (d. 1995) organized much of his later research agenda around the study of private, public, and Catholic education; he was particularly interested in exploring the social organization of these schools and its relationship to the academic success of students. In 1987, Coleman and Thomas Hoffer published the findings of their 1980 study *Public and Private High Schools: The Impact of Communities.* This study benchmarked what many Catholic educators knew intuitively, about the strong network of relationships between families, schools, church, and community which galvanized a unified resource that shared a common vision and set of goals in educating youth. Their data revealed that minority students, and those at risk for dropping out of school, were better served in Catholic schools because of the compensatory community resources supplied by social capital. If various support systems were missing in a student's home or community, Catholic schools, through their community and network of social capital, supplied the needed assets to students. These positive external forces have a beneficial impact upon the internal workings of a school's culture.[4]

Catholic schools cannot take anything for granted, and the belief that social capital continues to be a birthright many not always be the case. Just as people always presumed that sisters would be part of the educational landscape, new circumstances called upon other resources.

CHAPTER NINE

~

Lay Leadership Emerges

All of the theological insights of Vatican II were premised on the *universal call to holiness*, the concept that all the baptized have been given special graces and gifts to serve the Church and further the kingdom of Jesus. In many ways the role of the laity was to take the gospel uncompromised into their homes and workplace. Pope Benedict XVI reiterated this theme many times during his pastoral visit to the United States in April 2008.

While the juridical notion of a hierarchical church was never replaced, it was complemented with other images that emphasized roles and responsibilities for everyone. Sometimes various images and models of the Church are in conflict, but then the Church has rarely been without differing views of how best to proceed, even from the days of the apostles. Sometimes, those who desire a more egalitarian or democratic-type church have been frustrated when the leadership did not follow their hopes or agenda; it is doubtful it ever will, but certainly there is room for consultation, discussion, and better utilization of talented people.

This was especially recognized by the Sacred Congregation for Catholic Education when it issued the document *Lay Catholics in Schools: Witnesses to Faith* in 1982: "The most basic reason for this new role for Catholic laity, a role which the church regards as positive and enriching, is theological" (#2). The document roots this insight in various documents from Vatican II. *Lay Catholics in Schools: Witnesses to Faith* describes lay educational professionals in these words:

The teacher under discussion here is not simply a professional person who systematically transmits a body of knowledge in the context of a school; "teacher"
is to be understood as "educator"—one who helps to form human persons. The
task of a teacher goes well beyond transmission of knowledge, although that is not
excluded. Therefore, if adequate professional preparation is required in order to
transmit knowledge, then adequate professional preparation is even more necessary in order to fulfill the role of a genuine teacher. It is an indispensable human
formation, and without it, it would be foolish to undertake any educational work.

One specific characteristic of the educational profession assumes its most
profound significance in the Catholic educator: the communication of truth.
For the Catholic educator, whatever is true is a participation in Him who is
the Truth; the communication of truth, therefore, as a professional activity, is
thus fundamentally transformed into a unique participation in the prophetic
mission of Christ, carried on through one's teaching.[1]

This document clearly articulated a philosophy, vision, and appreciation
for those laymen and laywomen working in Catholic schools. It clearly enun-
ciated a positive attitude from the Church's leadership toward those who
labor in its schools. Many other Church documents, both from Rome and
those issued by particular national assemblies of bishops, would echo the esteem for those who serve as administrators and teachers in Catholic schools.

In 2005 the United States Conference of Catholic Bishops (USCCB) issued *Renewing Our Commitment to Catholic Elementary and Secondary Schools
in the Third Millennium*, a statement on Catholic education in which they not
only express their gratitude for the Catholic school system but also describe it
as a vital means of evangelization. They also describe the importance of faith
formation for those who will serve in leadership roles.

Ninety-five percent of our current school administrators and teachers are members of the laity. The preparation and ongoing formation of new administrators
and teachers is vital if our schools are to remain truly Catholic in all aspects of
school life. Catholic school personnel should be grounded in a faith-based Catholic culture, have strong bonds to Christ and the church, and be witnesses to the
faith in both their words and actions. The formation of personnel will allow the
Gospel message and the living presence of Jesus to permeate the entire life of
the school community and thus be faithful to the school's evangelizing mission.

We must provide a sufficient number of programs of the highest quality to
recruit and prepare our future diocesan and local school administrators and
teachers so that they are knowledgeable in matters of our faith, are professionally prepared, and are committed to the church. These programs will require
even more active involvement and cooperation by our Catholic colleges and
universities in collaboration with the diocesan educational leadership. Ongo-

ing faith formation and professional development programs must also be available so that administrators and teachers in Catholic schools can continue to grow in their ministry of education.[2]

As previously stated, most of the sisters imbued their elementary schools with the spiritual culture that was dominant at their motherhouse and particularly in the novitiates, since many left for teaching ministry immediately after professing simple vows. These lessons, customs, traditions, and rituals were simply done; there was not a manual or recipe book to describe this Catholic school culture. Hence for many laypeople who would follow a community of sisters, there might be quite a learning curve in trying to maintain a sense of continuity with the past, particularly if they had no experience either as a student or teacher in the Catholic school system in prior years.

Laypeople at the Helm

What may be most astonishing about laypersons moving into leadership in Catholic elementary schools is that their experience does not differ widely from that of the sisters. Even though there might have been some adjustments to a school without sisters, laypeople quickly focused upon the key mission of the school that was to impart an excellent education permeated with the Catholic faith. In reality most schools had some lay teachers throughout their history; it would be a very unique school that was completely staffed by sisters. It is good to recall that the pervasive presence of the religious sisters was not the original pattern. As Catherine and Robert Kealey explain in *On Their Shoulders: A Short Biographical History of American Catholic Schools* (2003):

> Lay men and women have been involved with Catholic schools since their inception. Mother Seton hired lay women to teach in her schools. The first school in New York had a lay faculty. When the Sisters of Mercy arrived in Savannah in 1845, six Catholic schools were already operating with completely lay staffs. Even in the mid-1960s, the period of the number and highest enrollment in Catholic schools, about one-third of the teachers were lay women and men. With the steady decline in the number of those religious orders over the last 40 years, the percentage of lay teachers has risen steadily. Today about ninety-two percent of Catholic school educators and administrators in the United States are lay women and men.[3]

A pastor might prefer a school completely staffed by sisters for many reasons; not least was the lower salaries, but sisters were also desired for the spirituality that was implied. In some larger schools there might be two rooms of each grade, or perhaps two full classes and then a split classroom. A sister and two laypersons or two sisters and one layperson might have been the teachers for these students. Sometimes parents preferred to have their children in the room of the sister when such a possibility, not a choice, was at hand.

In spite of this occasional preference, laypeople were professionals who were known and respected by the school families, and very often were their neighbors and friends in the parish. Hence, when they moved into a leadership role such as principal, it was not particularly jarring for people, but there was a difference.

One principal, "Robert Jones," recalled the transition at a school when the sisters announced in January their withdrawal at the end of the school. At the time Mr. Jones was serving as vice principal at "St. Barbara's" school. The sister principal alerted him of the coming disclosure prior to a faculty meeting and subsequent meeting with the parents.

Like other orders of women religious, the sisters serving at this school had taken stock of their future. Their diminishing numbers, lack of incoming vocations, openness to ministries other than education, and a renewed desire to serve the poor all converged to precipitate their withdrawal from this affluent parish. The most common reaction was put into a question: "Why are you doing this to us?"

There was a strong sentiment among the school families at St. Barbara's that the sisters embodied the Catholic culture of the school. People wondered how it could continue to be a Catholic school without the sisters, even though at the time of their withdrawal, there were only three still there. As the announcement fanned heated discussions, many speculated that the sisters' departure would also damage the enrollment.

Reflecting on the transition and the large shoes he was filling, Mr. Jones recalled a choice "to either be demoralized by being made to feel you were not quite an adequate replacement for sister, or to be determined to do the best job possible." He chose the latter. He remembered thinking about his response to the critics: "I'll show you! This experience got us to take a good look at our faith and be determined that the changes were an opportunity to be even better than we had been."

Perhaps this was a tactic to scare or manipulate the sisters into changing their minds, but it did not achieve its purpose. Indeed a few families withdrew, but there were multiple factors involved, and the easiest explanation would be to blame it on the sisters. However, with only three sisters working at the school, and one serving as principal, the odds favored a student having a layperson anyway as a teacher.

One of the sisters had traditionally served as the religion coordinator. Her duties included overseeing the catechetical program and various aspects of the spirituality of the school such as First Friday Masses and devotions, May crowning, Stations of the Cross, and rosary. Suddenly, these critical components of the school's culture, which had been taken for granted, would need leadership and a knowledge base, but the new lay principal was not going to let them disappear.

Mr. Jones recalled some of the sisters who were not supportive of the withdrawal from this parish still noted with confidence that the laity had been prepared for this transition: "We prepared you. We weaned you. You can do this, and do it well." Despite the pastor's frantic efforts to find another order of sisters to step into the school, he found that every other community was experiencing the same monumental shifts. At the end of that school year there was a bittersweet liturgy and reception for all the sisters who had ever taught at the school and for those in the area. Even after trying to absorb the departure, the general feeling of the parish was "Why are you doing this to us?"

Mr. Jones speculated on how the withdrawal of the sisters impacted the pastor and how it might have affected many priests and their attitudes toward Catholic schools. The withdrawal of the sisters and the impossibility of finding another community to work at the school introduced many new processes. First, it demanded the hiring of a principal and some kind of procedure to make that determination.

In the early days there was no hiring process—only the pastor's approval based upon who the sisters appointed from within the congregation. But with the rise of school boards, and more professional guidance from the chancery, the hiring of a new principal, lay or religious, developed into a more involved process, increasingly directed by the diocesan school office under the leadership of the school superintendent.

However, the departure of sisters from the schools signaled a new kind of relationship between the pastor and the parish school, and this usually took the form of more meetings—the bane of many parish priests. For years, pastors might have been able to defer to a sister principal to lead the school in its own matters, but a priest in the days of transition to lay leadership would often be seen as the sole religious authority. Until the laity had mastered a knowledge base, or developed a set of skills to lead the school, and felt the confidence to be spiritual leaders, there would be a need for the pastor's time and commitment to the school. Time and commitment were commodities as abundant or scarce as the priest's inclination.

One group of six laypersons who had all taught together at a large urban Catholic elementary school reflected upon their experience during a transition when the sisters left the school and one of the laity became principal. In fact, she became the first lay principal in that diocese. Most of these teachers had attended Catholic colleges for women and noted that there had been teachers in their own families, either their mothers or aunts. There seemed to be a positive tradition in teaching. All these women had families of their own, and at varying times they might have taken some time away from the classroom to raise their children.

This particular group all had working husbands, and their own income from teaching would have been supplementary; they were unanimous that the retirement benefits were terrible, if not scandalous, especially coming from a church that advocates for the rights and just treatment of the working person. Sometimes during their teaching careers, they might have spent time as substitute teachers especially when this worked better with family responsibilities. When they had retired from their teaching careers, a few continued to substitute teach. Each of them had taught full-time for close to twenty years and in one case, close to thirty. They recalled many of the details of the sisters leaving the school and how it impacted their own work and the culture of the school.

At the time they began teaching at this school, the sisters were clearly the leaders. All major decisions were made at the convent and then shared at the school with the other teachers and the staff. There was no apparent strife over this system; it was simply the way things were done, such as setting the calendar and scheduling. Many thought that since the sisters were together anyway, their time together meant they could figure out some of the details of the school, and it would be one less meeting to attend. In these days following Vatican II, there were no immediate expectations of collaboration or discussion. Catholics were accustomed to a regimented hierarchical dissemination of information.

When the leadership of the sisters had communicated to the pastor that they would need to withdraw, he was not happy with the decision. In fact, the pastor worked very hard to keep the sisters at the parish, but when it became apparent that the decision of the sisters was irreversible, he gradually started to consider an alternative approach.

He desperately sought another order of teaching sisters for the school. It was obvious as the 1960s unfolded into the 1970s that just about every teaching order of sisters was experiencing a diminishment of numbers due to retirement, departures from the community, and alternative ministries.

Anticipating the Challenges

The problem with how to staff parish schools without sisters was a concern at parishes across the country. In 1963 *Look* magazine ran the feature "Trouble Ahead for the Catholic Schools" by Jack Star, followed by the photo essay "The Vanishing Nun."[4]

The article describes the voracious demands of families for Catholic schools as outpacing the Church's ability to provide quality schools. Even with the large numbers of sisters entering religious life at the rate they were, it would be impossible to meet the demands of providing a sister in every classroom and a desk in a Catholic school for every student.

The growth of Catholic schools was an incredible success story; the demand for them is what Cardinal McIntyre was trying to address in Los Angeles. The bishops had argued the benefits of a Catholic education and encouraged parishes to build these institutions. The communities of sisters marshaled vast quantities of fiscal and human resources into the project with generosity and enthusiasm. The growing numbers of sisters who were entering religious life augured well for maintaining existing institutional commitments and provided a hope to open new schools and apostolates. But despite all their successes and optimistic indicators, problems were starting to fester.

Look author Jack Star quoted Donald McDonald, then the dean at Marquette University's College of Journalism, who described some of the increasing tensions in Catholic education:

> You find it and hear it, increasingly and with increasing intensity wherever and whenever Catholic parents get together privately and begin comparing notes on the quality of education their children are receiving. The notes are invariably identical. In parish after parish after parish, the elementary school is blighted by 70-, 80- and 90-pupil classrooms, overworked and harassed sister-teachers; split-shift classes; sub-marginally qualified and sub-marginally paid lay teachers pressed willy-nilly into classroom service.[5]

Star further outlined the growing gap between public schools and Catholic schools, and the lay teachers who worked in these schools:

> The Catholic schools are at a considerable disadvantage in competing with public schools for the available supply of lay teachers. Catholic elementary teachers are paid an average of only $3,400 a year, compared with over $5,200 for public schools. Hardly any Catholic school provides pension plans or periodic pay raises. It is therefore not surprising that, as one priest-researcher

concluded, Catholic "teachers do not have the numbers and kinds of academic degrees found among public-school teachers."[6]

Recall that many sisters who were fresh from the novitiate arrived at the schools without degrees or teaching credentials; these kinds of professional benchmarks were desired among Catholic educators but never mandated until recently. The Church in 1963 could not have conducted its schools with only the few people who were professionally prepared in state certified programs, as desirable as that might have been. Hence, the Church was satisfied with its mentoring system and those charismatically gifted people who were natural teachers. Much of this situation was on track to change, just as laypersons were beginning to move into the role of leadership conventionally held by priests and sisters. Star cited some of the tensions when he wrote,

> Lay educators are beginning to win top jobs as administrators. But William H. Conley, president of Sacred Heart University, in Bridgeport, Conn., comments that lay and religious teachers live in different worlds. They eat apart and talk over school problems apart. It is difficult, he says, to provide advancement for lay teachers "not only in salary but in positions of leadership. . . . Restricting the positions to the clergy or to a member of the religious community leads to the attitude that there is no future for the talented layman in the system."

Conley was understandably unaware of the drastic changes that were taking place at the very time he made these comments. Over the next fifteen years dramatic declines in the numbers of priests and sisters would cause a great need for lay leadership. It might take years for laywomen and laymen to penetrate the "stained-glass ceiling" within church schools, but it would happen, if not out of choice then increasingly out of necessity.

These observations of conflicts and tensions made in the midst of the Catholic school boom contradict the romantic notions that some people cultivate about the "good old days." John Cogley, a former executive editor of *Commonweal*, predicted in 1963 that Catholics would have to deal with many difficult dilemmas facing Catholic schools:

> The idea of nuns doing all the teaching is an extraordinary one, anyhow; it is less than a hundred years old, and it is certainly not Divine Revelation. The church is finding that education costs are astronomical and that it just can't compete with the state—it's a question of voluntary contributions versus taxes. I don't think the Catholic schools will disappear, but a larger and larger percentage of Catholic children just won't be going to Catholic schools. Yet we should not be too discouraged. The first purpose of a Catholic school was

soul-saving. But many Catholics now believe that its purpose is to develop an elite, articulate group of Catholics. Catholic education can certainly do that.[7]

It was into this changing world that the lay teachers would set a new course—not new in the sense of a new creation, but a new chapter in the culture of Catholic schools. All of these predictions unfolded. There were not enough nuns to meet the demands. Catholic schools did endure and have stood the test of time, despite diminishment in the number of schools and students. Catholic schools are not only concerned with the salvation of souls and evangelization but also eager to form responsible and active citizens who will take their place in society and the Church.

The More Things Change . . .

The relentless pressures caused by finances have also remained the greatest challenge to these schools. Laymen and laywomen, who are no strangers to fiscal planning and responsibility, stepped into this world at a time when their spirituality and practical sense of business may have been needed most.

Laywoman Annabel McInerney, who had been the first lay principal at her school of St. Elizabeth's School in Kansas City, Missouri, after being a successful middle school teacher, shared these recollections: She felt that the sisters, the pastor, and other leaders had prepared the people for the transition. She was known and well respected in the parish, and she developed an excellent working relationship with the pastor. Like so many sisters, this principal was able to speak about her work with the pastor. She felt supported and encouraged by him, and it was evident to the parishioners that she not only had the necessary administrative graduate degree but also the teaching credentials. Her transition was fairly smooth and seamless, but the teachers had a curious experience.

When the sisters had staffed St. Elizabeth's School, in addition to their teaching duties during the week, they also ran the Confraternity of Christian Doctrine, or CCD, on the weekends. Every parish in the United States has a CCD program offering religion classes for those students who attend public schools. In some cities, students in public schools might have had release time from public school to attend these weekly religion classes at the parish. However, these classes were often taught on Saturday or Sunday mornings, or possibly during the evening in the middle of the week.

It has been a perpetual challenge to get students motivated for these classes, especially if they fell on a Saturday morning. Regardless of the scheduling, these classes gave teachers an extra block of time for preparation and delivery of instruction. The sisters would try to condense as much of a week's instruction into that brief time each week, while trying to motivate and engage the students.

A typical challenge consisted of getting children to prepare for the classes, motivating them, and keeping them engaged for the year. Parents also faced battles in getting children to engage in catechesis, tearing them away from Saturday morning cartoons, sports, or other recreation. It was, and is still, a monumental challenge to deliver excellent catechesis, making it attractive and not like another day of school.

The sisters at St. Elizabeth's worked weekends. When they left, the question before the pastor was, *who would fulfill the role of CCD teachers?* The pastor determined the course the school would take and commissioned his deacon to inform the school staff of his decision. At this particular school, the longtime kindergarten teacher always hosted a luncheon at her home on the last day of school since her class was dismissed before the rest of the school. The deacon acting as the pastor's emissary chose this celebratory gathering with the teachers to tell them of the unique opportunity they had. The pastor wanted these lay teachers to not only continue the excellent work of the sisters during the week by conducting the school but also run the CCD program on the weekend.

The teachers were flabbergasted with this plan. The deacon presented this request with enthusiasm and confidence that the faculty would gladly accept the additional duties, but a new day was slowly dawning in the church. In fact, the teachers were required to accept additional duties according to a clause the pastor had placed in their contracts. So if they wanted their jobs for that coming year, they had to accept this additional teaching duty.

The news was met with absolute silence; the teachers were absolutely astounded by this demand. Carol Lynn, who had been substituting that day and was present at the luncheon, broke the icy silence: "I spoke up and said that I thought it was a great idea. Since I had been a CCD teacher and most of those teachers did a poor job, I thought the full-time teachers would do a much better job. Everyone glared at me!"

The teachers did accept the added responsibilities for that coming year, but another arrangement would have to be developed for the future. The teachers had families and duties that precluded them from teaching in the CCD program. It is interesting to note that while the personnel had changed at the school with the departure of the sisters, the attitude toward the teachers had not changed that much.

Many new situations would arise that would need discussion in the wake of sisters leaving the parishes. There were countless jobs they performed that often went unnoticed. This could not have been an isolated experience. The wisdom of having the sisters teach the CCD students was that a unified catechetical experience was extended to all the children of the parish; they would also benefit from the leadership and contact with the sisters of the parish. However, this would be another area in the parish where the gifts of the laity would need to be enlisted more.

It is an unfortunate truth that there is often tension between a CCD program and the Catholic school of a parish. The CCD students would usually have their classes in the parish elementary school. Teachers and students enrolled in the school would frequently complain that the classrooms were left in disarray or things would be missing. CCD families would complain that they felt like second-class citizens in the parish. It is a very difficult situation because it is impossible to impart in one lesson a week what is woven into a full week of school. At one parish, a sister served as director of the CCD program. She was an untiring advocate for the children in her program. Concerned that the CCD children were not being treated well, she visited the classrooms of the school. One teacher who welcomed a classroom visitation recalled that the sister asked what could be done to remedy the problems between the CCD students and school children. One little girl said, "We can make them feel welcome." To this, the sister snapped, "Who are you to welcome them? This place doesn't belong to you. They could just as easily welcome you." The teacher was initially pleased with the girl's response but was then embarrassed for all involved.[8]

The story illustrates a regrettable but real tension that exists in many parishes between the CCD program and the parish school. Yet the vast majority of the Church's children are in public schools and in need of excellent catechesis. More than anything, it highlights an area in need of work and collaboration.

After Vatican II, dioceses developed well-intentioned, though seriously misguided, programs to help form catechists; unfortunately, these efforts ushered in a period of religious illiteracy that converged with untold foolishness masquerading as catechesis, and these were not exclusively found in CCD programs but also in Catholic schools (Greeley and Rossi, 1966). This was a time when students made felt banners to fill the sacred spaces vacated by statuary or religious images carried away by the iconoclasts; secular and banal folk music replaced Palastrina, Mozart, and Gregorian Chant. Pop psychology and the cult of the priest's personality and performance were on the ascendancy (Day, 1990). The Baltimore Catechism was replaced with various textbook series that were characterized as vapid and questionable, or stories like *The Little Prince* and *The Velveteen Rabbit* were read at the liturgy instead of the scriptures, since they were supposedly more relevant.

As the Church tried to find its way to a place of balance, there were many silly seasons to be endured with clown ministry, homilies with props, puppets, gimmicks, and endless liturgical folderol. What might be a proof of God's existence was that people continued to believe and participate in the life of the Church even during these dark days of experimentation. Most amazingly, they returned to the scene of the crime week after week, usually putting money in the collection basket.

Continuity and Untold Problems

Just as the lay teachers at the aforementioned school encountered stumbling blocks with their new roles, around the country lay teachers and leaders faced challenges as the sisters left the schools. One lay principal on the East Coast walked into a nightmare of transition when she followed "Sister Estelle," who had been principal for thirty years. The sisters of this community had served at this parish for well over one hundred years. Not only had this sister been revered and respected by the families of the parish, but she would also remain at the school supervising Marian devotions and other activities in the school while serving as a mentor to the new principal "Meredith Breseau."

"It was a very difficult situation," Mrs. Breseau reported. During Sister Estelle's time as principal, she had hired many non-degreed people, a trend that has all but disappeared from Catholic schools. Though these were always well-intentioned people, and sometimes very fine teachers, it was a reality that no school could continue this practice with rising professional standards. The school building was in ramshackle shape, with an antiquated phone system. However, the best feature of the phones was the ability of the principal to eavesdrop from the convent into the office.

Sister Estelle was pleased with the appointment of Mrs. Breseau because she felt this laywoman would continue practices that had been in place for thirty years, including corporal punishment. While people were petrified of Sister Estelle, they also admired her; she was an institution.

Sister Estelle was described by the new principal as being helpful with documents, forms, and other administrative tasks, but when there were efforts to make changes, mischief was unleashed. Changes, such as paint colors for classrooms and updated uniforms, became points of contention with an undercurrent of dissension. Some long-neglected increases in tuition paralleled a drop in enrollment.

As the school was being strengthened through new leadership, some of the changes were not easily accepted. Mrs. Breseau permitted women to wear slacks, a revolutionary decision that was being second-guessed by the presence of the revered and retired Sister Estelle. Working in the shadow of a popular predecessor is never easy. It is a rare individual who can remain associated with a school after relinquishing responsibilities and not be a lightning rod for controversy.

In this case, people would immediately flock to the former principal whenever they did not like the way things were going. As Mrs. Breseau described, "It was hard to be your own person with one's predecessor hovering over you and getting entangled in every issue at the school."

She saw a complex web of relationships between the convent, rectory, and school: "The laity are typically shut out of many decisions. We are vulnerable to the whims and personalities of leadership. How can you lead a school when it is not clear if you are being supported?"

The tensions were not just between the convent, which was physically connected to the school, and the educational project. This maelstrom included the rectory as well. People were able to shop for solutions at three different stops until they found a resolution to their liking. In the chain of command this principal was at the bottom. This sad story clearly illustrates the need for a working or functional team of all the leaders.

Clearly, the retired principal should have been missioned elsewhere; this was a failure on the part of the congregation's leadership to see what would benefit the apostolate. However, these sisters were under an open-placement system, and having been assigned to the parish for so long, it might have seemed cruel to ask this sister to move. But the leadership team should have known this religious, and while acknowledging her strengths and weaknesses, they should have placed the success of the school's new leader above the desires of one sister.

While a religious who happens to stay at an assignment for a long period may offer a great deal of continuity to families, longevity also brings untold problems. Most dioceses have term limits for priests serving in parishes because both the people and the priests need a change. When religious stay too long in one assignment, intransigence is often a companion. New members of the community are forced to conform to whims that have been set in stone. Religious can also become inflexible and beyond reproach. Superiors will find such religious resistant to any kind of change, and each passing year will atrophy the person that much more as the creative energies become fossilized.

Indeed, many religious provincials have lamented that their greatest problem is the unavailability for mission among a community's members. Sisters, brothers, and priests will appeal to their effective ministry about how the work they are doing is so important and will fall apart without their personal leadership and presence. Messianic complexes are quite common among religious, especially those who have held on to positions of power and authority well beyond a reasonable term or two. For just about any religious who has been associated with a Catholic institution for an unusually long time, and who has earned the affection of being "an institution," you can be most certain that there is another, less rosy side of the story, as in the case of Sister Estelle, who had been principal for thirty years and was continuing as a "mentor" and manipulator.

Mrs. Breseau learned some important lessons about power and leadership. When Sister Estelle died—while still assigned to the community at the parish convent—there was a large wake and funeral for her. However, there were endless comparisons of how things used to be when Sister Estelle was principal. Nonetheless, the diocesan superintendent of schools praised Mrs. Breseau, telling her that the school had never seen such active leadership or such good practices being implemented under her direction.

CHAPTER TEN

~

Transition and Signs of Renewal

The gradual or sudden departure of women religious from Catholic elementary schools is now a part of the historical record. Those with a living memory of these schools with the presence of sisters often cherish their memories and the positive influence that the sisters had upon their lives and faith formation. Today, there are many schools that have sisters working in them but, as was pointed out at the beginning of the book, and contrary to the popular cultural imagination, most Catholic elementary schools do not have sisters teaching in them.

It is hard to imagine that this trend will ever reverse itself to any approximation of the past. However, there are orders of sisters that continue to get large numbers of young women entering each year as novices and persevering in their vocations; these orders tend to share a commitment to Catholic education, according to the *Recent Vocations to Religious Life: A Report for the National Religious Vocation Conference*. This 2009 study described people who had recently joined religious life. Many of the findings point toward a growth or stability in those communities that chose the traditional route described in chapter 6. The indicators seem to augur well for communities who have maintained a strong commitment to Catholic schools.

Orders such as Sisters of St. Francis of the Martyr St. George in Alton, Illinois; the Dominican Sisters of Mission San José in San José, California; the Apostles of the Sacred Heart of Jesus in Hamden, Connecticut; the Dominican Sisters of Nashville in Tennessee; the Dominican Sisters of Mary Mother of the Eucharist in Michigan; and the Franciscan Sisters of

Christian Charity in Manitowoc, Wisconsin, are examples of communities with strong ties to schools.

It is precisely this kind of religious witness that has diminished from much of the landscape of American Catholicism. In a not-too-distant past, sisters were a great part of the Church where it met most people—that is, in the parishes. The transition was well described by Suellen Hoy (2006) in *Good Hearts: Catholic Sisters in Chicago's Past*:

> "Convent" is what the small, chiseled sign said. I noticed it one Sunday afternoon not long ago, as my husband and I were walking to our car on Chicago Avenue. I stopped, turned to him, and asked: "When was the last time you saw a sign like that?" We couldn't remember. Convents are hard to find today, even though during much of the twentieth century they numbered in the hundreds. Once familiar anchors of Chicago's neighborhoods, most of them—along with many schools and churches—are now closed or used for other purposes. On a rare occasion, though, you may come across a convent that still houses a few Catholic sisters.[1]

Hoy's observation is not only descriptive of the city of Chicago but also one that could be used for cities across the United States. The sisters are not as present, and many of the convents have been converted to parish offices, day care centers, or other functions for the parish, if they have not been sold outright. Another popular myth in the minds of Catholics is that there are abundant convents waiting to be used for other purposes. The PLACE Corps (Partners in Los Angeles Catholic Education), a partnership program between the Archdiocese of Los Angeles and Loyola Marymount University, offers an instructive example.

The PLACE Corps is composed of recent college graduates, young men and women who teach at underresourced Catholic elementary and secondary schools for two years. While teaching and living in the community, they are also pursuing a master's degree in education and their teaching credentials. There are many schools willing and eager to hire and mentor these novice teachers. There are plentiful numbers of generous men and women seeking to enter the program. The greatest obstacle that the program faces is finding adequate housing for the participants. Diana Murphy, the executive director of the PLACE Corps, is frequently advised to use some of "those empty convents that no longer house nuns." In fact, many of the PLACE Corps communities live in former convents, but there simply are not as many former convents available as people might think, and they are not thorn-free arrangements, according to Murphy:

Aside from finding the initial convent housing . . . the biggest and ongoing problem—is convent maintenance, repair, and renovation. Just like a personal residence or some form of campus housing, there is a constant need to repair and keep the places up. (We have had shredded carpets and shredded drapes, cracked flooring and tubs/showers whose caulking gave up functionality decades ago, faucets that had minds of their own, new locks and keys. Lighting that died and security lighting needed. Gates and fences to repair. . . . Appliance repair/replacement is another story.)

Determining what comes under "landlord" and what does not is another chapter. Of course, we are in poor parishes. While the pastor or landlord may appreciate that we "serve"—many consider the PLACErs as rent paying residents that may be more trouble than they're worth. We are constantly concerned with longevity of our arrangements and hate to invest in property that does not belong to us, property that we may not even be living in a few years down the road. The landlords receive nominal rent per person which is more than they would get otherwise because these places are not generally rentable (to nonreligious groups) due to zoning issues. If not renting to PLACE, the parishes have vacant convents in limbo or have found parish or school use for the former convents. Meanwhile the rent is not major income when all is said and done.[2]

The presence and leadership of laity in Catholic education continues to increase. The future of Catholic schools will be guided and formed by their gifts and passion for the ministry of education. These developments are certainly rooted in the vision of Vatican II. As *Lumen Gentium*, the dogmatic constitution on the Church, described:

The lay apostolate, however, is a participation in the salvific mission of the Church itself. Through their baptism and confirmation all are commissioned to that apostolate by the Lord Himself. Moreover, by the sacraments, especially holy Eucharist, that charity toward God and man which is the soul of the apostolate is communicated and nourished. Now the laity are called in a special way to make the Church present and operative in those places and circumstances where only through them can it become the salt of the earth. Thus every layman, in virtue of the very gifts bestowed upon him, is at the same time a witness and a living instrument of the mission of the Church itself "according to the measure of Christ's bestowal."

Besides this apostolate which certainly pertains to all Christians, the laity can also be called in various ways to a more direct form of cooperation in the apostolate of the Hierarchy. This was the way certain men and women assisted Paul the Apostle in the gospel, laboring much in the Lord. Further, they have the capacity to assume from the Hierarchy certain ecclesiastical functions, which are to be performed for a spiritual purpose.

Upon all the laity, therefore, rests the noble duty of working to extend the divine plan of salvation to all men of each epoch and in every land. Consequently, may every opportunity be given them so that, according to their abilities and the needs of the times, they may zealously participate in the saving work of the Church.[3]

This quote demonstrates a great confidence in the gifts and abilities of the laity. While clearly asserting the apostolic leadership responsibilities of the hierarchy, the bishops also describe the importance of calling upon the laity to assist them in appropriate domains of expertise. This may be an area that needs greater cultivation within the Church, but there is no better place to apply the expertise of the laity than in Catholic schools.

Every Catholic school, for at least the past forty years, has operated with a large number of laypersons, and would have closed long ago if institutional life was premised on the sole contributions of religious. Those religious in the trenches of ministry are quite well versed in the valuable contributions of the laity. The laity represent the lion's share of the Church's workforce and these disciples have their own gifts. In fact, some new emerging models of lay participation in education mirror the generous contributions to Catholic schools that were embodied for so many generations by women religious.

New Initiatives

The University of Notre Dame's Alliance for Catholic Education (ACE) was established in 1993 to provide teachers to underresourced Catholic schools, primarily in Southern states. Through ACE young people volunteer two years of service while pursuing graduate teaching degrees and state credentials. It is an intense experience of academic and professional training. Notre Dame has helped many other Catholic colleges and universities to establish programs throughout the United States, including Partners in Los Angeles Catholic Education (PLACE) Corps, a partnership program between the Archdiocese of Los Angeles and Loyola Marymount University.

These fourteen programs from across the country form the University Consortium for Catholic Education. Some of the new teachers stay at their assigned schools after they complete the program, and many others remain in other Catholic schools or in the teaching profession. Some students who have taught for several years are now moving into administration. Unlike the sisters who pursued their degrees and credentials on the "twenty-year plan," these students are in a twenty-month program.

These programs are a source of great pride and distinction in their home dioceses and also in the universities that house them. These efforts, which strive to recruit outstanding young Catholic role models as teachers, represent the kind of collaboration called for by Pope John Paul II in his 1990 apostolic constitution on higher education, *Ex corde ecclesiae*. Among the many points he articulated was the importance of the universities working with the local church together in mission.

Not surprisingly, these programs all seem to renew and enliven the faith of their participants. It is presumed that the Catholic participants be active and practicing members of the church. Many had been leaders in pastoral and service activities as undergraduates. Among the application materials is an autobiography that includes reflections about their faith life. They are also asked to present a letter of recommendation from someone who can address their spiritual readiness and maturity as a teacher in a Catholic school.

Many of these students represent the best and brightest of what Catholic education is producing. However, these programs also sometimes have young people who are indifferent or confused about their faith commitment; some lack an age-appropriate catechetical foundation. Lack of committed and intelligent Catholics will undermine a Catholic school, so vigilance in recruitment is critical for these programs.

On the whole, though, it is encouraging to know that these young people are the new leaders for Catholic schools and will provide competency, vision, and energy. It is gratifying to form strong lay leaders, and it is also heartening to see that some of the graduates have entered the seminary and religious life.

Advice from the Sisters about Leadership Transition

One thing we've learned from history is that we do *not* learn from history: we continue to make the same or similar mistakes as our predecessors and fail to heed the hard-won experience of others. Nonetheless, many helpful suggestions have been offered by the women and men, religious and lay, who witnessed firsthand the monumental changes in the Catholic schools over the past sixty years. No advice or set of procedures can fully ameliorate the pain that often comes with change, but some thoughtful preparation can make the change agent's job easier.

Follow Procedures
Regardless of whether religious orders use an open-placement system that relies upon individual initiative or a system whereby the community generates

assignments, there is generally a great deal of conversation about the assign-ment, the person, and the fit. Most religious communities use a collaborative model of governance, whereby consultation is a part of every decision and information about the process is shared.

Some problems and misunderstandings arose from leaders not following the directives and protocols that a community had agreed upon. Therefore, a primary and fundamental step would be to follow any procedure that is in place. "Sister Timothy" commented on the abrupt announcement and with-drawal of her community from a school, "There was a process but the process was not followed."

Be Transparent within the Limits of Confidentiality

Along with following the protocols that address specific situations, there is the need for these procedures to be known and transparent. Transparency is a value and habit that everyone appreciates, but some sensitive information must be held in confidentiality.

The case of the sisters withdrawing from a parish primarily due to the cantankerous pastor is instructive. The sisters respected the office of the pastor and had great affection for those serving as priests. When it became clear that the community had reached the end of its options, they discreetly withheld information that could be misunderstood or harmful to the reputa-tion of the parish and school.

Subsidiarity: Solve Problems at the Lowest Levels

Subsidiarity is the theory that asserts that matters are best handled at their lowest levels by the people involved with a question, and only when these diplomatic negotiations are totally exhausted does one approach the next higher rung of authority. Parents utilize this strategy with quarreling children when the parents do not want to settle every argument and the siblings are admonished to solve their own problems.

Perhaps the best illustration of this comes from Father Thomas Sherman, SJ, a university Jesuit who worked in a jail on weekends. A female convict was very upset that no one was bringing her the Eucharist, so she wrote a let-ter to Pope John Paul II complaining about the situation. Many people might be led to think that such mail gets dropped into an ecclesial black hole at the Vatican, but this missive did arrive in Rome.

The letter was then sent from Rome to the bishop at the chancery office in the diocese where the jail was located, requesting a remedy to the woman's complaint. The bishop then dispatched this request to the chaplain in charge of prison ministry, who informed Father Sherman about the situation. Upon investigation, the woman was not receiving the Eucharist because she was not Catholic and so did not appear on their list. Had she made a simple inquiry to the prison chaplain or authorities there, the question could have been easily addressed, but since the only Catholic she knew by name was the pope in Rome, that was the route her complaint took; this story illustrates an extreme example of what subsidiarity is not.[4]

At the parish with a difficult pastor, the sister who was known as an experienced troubleshooter with complicated personalities and situations attempted to deal with the responsible person. Recall that she had been preceded by other members of her community who had tried to resolve the problems between the rectory and the school. Her report to the provincial house described an intractable set of problems with an obstinate leader.

This case demonstrates the value of working from the bottom to the top. Those who are on the scene are much more knowledgeable of a situation than those in some other part of the country or world. When information has been successfully gathered and attempts to address the problem have been exhausted, then a higher authority can successfully intervene and continue to build upon the work that has already been done.

If the dynamics of subsidiarity are not followed, and the higher authority does arbitrate the situation, it is unlikely that the parties will welcome the remedy with open arms. Making time for appropriate consultation and collaboration are essential to changing a situation.

Allow Sufficient Time—But Not Too Much

Having ample time to study a tenuous commitment at a school, then having time for the appropriate stakeholders to confer about the findings and make, absorb, and implement a decision to leave is essential. Such time is always subjective, and it is doubtful that there would ever be a sufficient amount of time to make a hard decision to leave an assignment any more palatable.

As described previously, the sisters who had to withdraw from a school went through the typical stages of bereavement. "Sister Margaret" said leaving a school had aspects of "a divorce, sudden death, or wake." Another sister observed that while the sisters themselves were going through stages of mourning, they were also called upon to help others through their grief.

Often, what people may be hoping for is to avoid the realities and the grief work that must accompany an inevitable decision. No one willingly seeks out the way of the cross, but the paschal mystery holds the light and promise of renewal. People do need time to process decisions, and to the degree that it is possible, leadership should carefully consider a timeline that respects all that must be done.

Undoubtedly there are innumerable points that leadership must consider when making major decisions, but the gift of time cannot be underestimated. Sister Diana, who directed the withdrawal at two schools, observed that transition periods should have been better calculated and increased, yet she also concluded that even with more time, there would have been the same hard feelings and difficulties.

Of course, sometimes there can be too much time during a departure, and that does not serve the project either. Protracted exits are unwise. Sister Mary Peter Traviss, OP, recalled arrangements whereby one sister would be withdrawn each year until the final remaining sister had left. This method was extremely difficult for everyone, especially the sisters.

There may have been a financial edge given to the parish in being able to plan for the financial increase of a layperson's salary, but the psychological and social stresses on the sisters were considerable. Once a difficult decision has been made, it might be best to implement it quickly. To prolong the inevitable can give time for grousing and endless speculation, which will probably not be helpful.

Once a hard decision has been made, the healing and renewal can begin, even though these initial stages will be marked by disequilibrium, disbelief, anger, bargaining, and avoidance.

Ritualize Change

Catholicism values rituals. Rituals allow us to put a fine point on what we deem significant and worthy of our undivided attention, including rites of passage or other achievements and transitions. Thus, it was natural that when sisters left parishes, there were numerous ways to express appreciation and bid farewell through liturgies, dinners, and formal receptions.

Rituals can also be used to create bonds and identify what the school holds in esteem. A lay principal described her first impression upon entering her new school: one saw three large trophy cases displaying over twenty-five years of athletic awards. Upon reflection, she realized that the message this was conveying was that sports were the most important activity at the school. She decided to rearrange the focus of the cases. Each case would display awards or activities at the school. One case was dedicated to mission and service, one was for academics, and one was for sports.

Catholic schools abound with significant visual symbols that include the crucifix, statues of the Blessed Virgin Mary, and other reminders of the school's spiritual legacy and its relationship with the church. Numerous rituals can be found in all Catholic schools, such as weekly Mass attendance, penance services during Advent and Lent, and the celebration of Catholic Schools Week each January.

Individual schools might also have other devotions or activities specific to them, such as a celebration on the feast day of the saint after which the school is named or specific devotions reflective of the charism or mission of the religious community that continues to be connected to the school. Of course, all schools have academic and athletic award ceremonies to ritualize achievement and graduation.

Contemporary research on organizational strategies reinforces the importance of ritual and symbol that has been an enduring part of Catholic school culture. In *Reframing Organizations: Artistry, Choice, and Leadership* (2003), Lee Bolman and Terrence Deal describe the "symbolic frame of leadership," whereby leaders build team spirit through ritual ceremony and story, and shape a culture that gives purpose and meaning to the work of the organization.

Put Structures in Place for Mentoring and Succession

Just as the sisters who moved from the novitiate to the classrooms had mentors, Catholic schools today also need good structures for mentoring. All schools will experience a turnover in leadership; a tenure of ten years is a good benchmark for any leader to share his or her expertise, but beyond that, both the leader and the school will need a change, despite a harmonious organizational culture. Leaders should always be sharing information and responsibilities to diminish unhealthy aspects of dependency.

While leaders cannot conduct their work with a sense that they could leave at any minute, succession planning may alleviate any fears or instability. Clearly, a principal who has been on the job for a number of years and is doing an excellent job will bring stability to the school and build confidence in the organization. However, having contracts or letters of intent that state a definite period of time that one is likely to serve provides an urgency to accomplish goals within that timeframe.

In addition, a cooperative school environment that has consistently mentored new leadership and shared leadership responsibilities will certainly be able to absorb major changes more peacefully than those schools where duties and information were restricted to one person.

These points not only apply to schools led by sisters but also to schools staffed exclusively by the laity. It is not uncommon for an elementary school to suddenly find itself needing to replace a third or half of its faculty in a single year. Pregnancies, relocation of a family, illness, retirement, and moves to the public school system are all plausible and well-known reasons why there might be a convergence of departures in a single year, requiring a major effort in hiring and maintaining the mission and culture of a school.

Age can also play a role in major shifts in Catholic elementary school faculties. It is almost as if a cohort of peers is marching to the same chronological beat, which may precipitate a number of simultaneous departures. A group that all began teaching fresh out of college, then married about the same time and started raising families, may all be on the same career trajectory. At the other end of the career spectrum, older faculty members may need time off to care for aging parents, ill spouses, or themselves. Whatever circumstances hasten departures, it is not unusual to have these transitions occur in clusters.

In most schools, shortly after Christmas break, faculty are requested to indicate whether they intend to continue teaching and desire to sign a contract for the coming school year so that the principal can begin to plan the budget and hire faculty and staff. This is also done in concert with polling families about their intent to enroll their students for the coming year. While last-minute problems will still arise in schools with good mentoring and succession planning, these approaches can help minimize the difficulties of inevitable periods of transition.

Despite all the best planning in the world and following every imaginable protocol for change and incorporating ample time, problems arise. Every principal can recount their own nightmares and horror stories that serve as exceptions to sound leadership procedures. Despite the fact that teachers sign binding legal contracts, it would be a rare principal who did not discover days or hours before the first day of school that a particular teacher was not going to honor the contract. Again, the reasons for such a last-minute retreat are as diverse as the persons who make those fateful phone calls or send a letter of notification. Obviously, there are reasons that are understandable, such as when a teacher has had an emergency situation develop in his or her life or family; such circumstances are treated with understanding and compassion.

Finding a teacher before the first day of school throws a principal's opening of school preparations totally off kilter. Though the teacher who defaults on such a contract is liable, it is probably unheard of that anyone has ever been prosecuted for breach of this contract. Like trying to collect unpaid tuition, a principal and pastor are hard pressed by both time and financial constraints to seek a remedy for failure to comply with a contract. Further, what good would be served by forcing someone who did not want to be working at a particular school to accept the demands of such a contract? One could easily imagine the miserable climate and culture that such ill and toxic feelings would foster in the school and particularly in the classroom.

While endless preparations can be made for any school year, a healthy understanding of chaos theory, described so well by Margaret Wheatley in *Leadership and the New Science: Discovering Order in a Chaotic World* (1992), would be a wise lesson to have as background music. Wheatley asserts that when organizations experience unpredictable periods of turbulence, over time, science demonstrates that patterns are discernible, but most likely not in the heat of the day when such a flashpoint has flared. The lesson for the leader is to know intuitively that unforeseen changes and circumstances are part of the job. A great deal of any principal or leader's time is spent solving problems in addition to planning and structuring the normal thrust of a school year. Perhaps it is the careful planning of so many ordinary things that allows the leader to respond to the crises and tribulations that inevitably accompany the presence of at least one or two other people.

CHAPTER ELEVEN

~

The Future of Catholic Schools and the Legacy of the Sisters

"Sister Maria" observed that it is almost impossible to fully prepare for the withdrawal of sisters from a school. No matter how much preparation or time is ascribed to the process, a difficult transition awaits the parish:

> There was really no preparation for this transition. We did, however, have a mission statement in place that included some sense of our charism. Although parents decried this decision, they were aware of the fact that vocations were few, and this impacted some of the decision to leave this parish school.

Some schools have attempted to retain a relationship with the community of sisters that had served them. This approach shows a forward thinking initiative on the part of a community to recognize that while they cannot offer a workforce, there are ways to creatively cultivate a relationship and presence at the school. The Sisters of St. Joseph of Orange, California, have maintained such bonds.

This congregation established the Educational Network in 1988 to serve as a resource for Catholic schools, especially, though not limited to, those schools where the congregation has served. The Educational Network offers many services, including professional development and consultation services for administration, curriculum development, leadership development, ministerial development, and help with mission effectiveness.

A Proposal to Women Religious

Nearly every congregation of sisters that has served in the educational apostolate has scores of talented and experienced leaders and teachers. If a congregation for myriad reasons no longer has sisters available to staff a school, they might consider other ways to contribute to the educational works of the Church. While there is no substitute for a group of sisters in the school, there are other ways to imagine "presence" and help a school. A community's collective understanding of teaching skills and leadership could provide an effective resource that is going untapped. Many leaders at struggling Catholic schools feel isolated. Having a relationship with a religious community and its heritage would contribute to the stability and excellence of a school.

It would be invaluable if every community produced a collection of tips gleaned from their members. Practical instructions could focus on teaching, administration, discipline, catechetics, working with families, fundraising, community-building, and so on. Perhaps a community could appoint a sister or team of sisters in the spirit of the former education supervisors who would offer professional development. The Sisters of St. Joseph of Orange have provided an excellent model for maintaining presence and involvement in Catholic schools. Let us hope other communities will follow.

A Proposal to Researchers

Some communities have begun conducting interviews with their retired members to have a record of these members. Researchers might consider gathering the administrative and teaching wisdom of women religious. This large group of teaching sisters is a living library of important lessons that could enhance Catholic schools and spur professional development of leaders and teachers.

Catholic Universities and Leadership Programs

Another important step toward ensuring healthy Catholic schools has been the conscious effort of colleges and universities to offer these schools professional preparation programs. Catholic Higher Education Supporting Catholic Schools (CHESCS, pronounced "chess") exists for this purpose and offers master's degrees in administration among other programs designed to prepare leaders for Catholic schools. Its member institutions work closely with the local dioceses and Catholic school offices. Generally these schools may offer one of the following programs or a combination: master's degrees in elementary or secondary teaching, master's degrees in Catholic school administration, or doctorates (EdD or PhD) that specialize in some aspect of leadership. Most of the programs offered are in the area of administration.

Many of the sisters interviewed for this book offered advice related to academic preparation. One sister witnessed many excellent lay educators moving from public schools into the Catholic school system as principals. While acknowledging their skills and abilities, she also noted some challenges: "Lay people who have not taught in Catholic schools should spend some time getting familiar with the Christian presence. There are differences that need to be discovered about respect and acceptance."

Another sister, who continues to serve in Catholic education for her community and is very committed to the poor, felt it was important "to maintain stability in schools after sisters withdraw. A key to that is to be sure that the leadership is well-grounded in their faith and knows how to share it with others and how to receive it from others."

These observations underscore an earlier point that the culture of Catholic elementary schools was substantially imported from the novitiate and the motherhouse. Many lay educators have not formally studied their faith or theology since secondary school, let alone the foundations of Catholic education. Nor can one presume that an undergraduate education at a Catholic university confers any theological edge.

Sound pedagogy and administrative competencies are of universal value in every school. But in a Catholic school, many strategies assume a greater importance and have a deeper significance because the Catholic mission will permeate every decision, lesson, and program—if not objectively, then most likely in the intentionality or style in which something is done.

It's a Catholic School: Let's Keep It Catholic (2005), by Sister Edward William Quinn, IHM, offers excellent strategies and tips for work in this area, including models to enhance the Catholic identity of every school through communal prayers, classroom environment, celebrations, curriculum, and global outreach.

Knowledge and Skills for Catholic School Leaders

The knowledge base for Catholic school leadership should include topics such as private school law and ethics, catechetical leadership, foundations of Catholic education, leadership and administration in Catholic education, and finance and management. Beyond some of the technical and practical knowledge, it could help lay leaders to have a rich encounter with the history of Catholic education in the United States and an introduction to the ecclesial documents that shape the philosophical mission of the schools. Here are some essentials for every Catholic school leader.

Be Familiar with Church Teaching on Education

For many people this will provide an excellent opportunity to read and reflect upon the educational ministry of the Church, especially as it has developed over the past two centuries and particularly as it has flourished in the United States. It is principally the encyclicals, *motu proprios*, decrees, and episcopal letters that convey the rich, spiritual sense of the educational apostolate (see appendix B).

Remember, Parents Are the Primary Educators of Their Children

Foundational Catholic attitudes are cultivated in these documents, such as the parents being the primary educators of their children. As such, the parents should be free and have the support to choose the school that will best serve the needs of their family. Traditionally, the Catholic school has been seen as an auxiliary or partner with the parents to support the lessons of faith and morals being taught in the home, while offering the other academic disciplines in a manner informed by the Catholic faith.

Educate the Whole Person

A central theme all these documents share is the ministry of educating the whole person. The readings also emphasize the spiritual and catechetical development of young people. But what many educators find inspiring and consoling are the solicitous words of gratitude that are repeatedly expressed for the men and women who respond to the call to serve in the ministry of education. These documents are aimed at education in the public and private realms, but they are also directed to Catholic school leaders.

Demonstrate Exemplary Teaching Skills

Generally, principals are selected from the teaching ranks by demonstrating excellent teaching and/or organizational skills; they will become the teacher of the teachers, finding and offering professional development, as well as observing, coaching, and supervising the faculty and staff. While being an excellent teacher doesn't guarantee the skill set needed to be a good principal, a school's faculty provides the talent pool from which administrators are sought. Within the classroom, a teacher must demonstrate extraordinary organizational skills in planning, delivering, and assessing lessons.

Teachers Are Chief Motivators and Models

Teachers must also serve as motivators, encouraging a wide range of abilities to achieve their very best, even when students and families may be uncooperative or attempt to undermine the educational project. Teachers serve as judges, pondering decisions and meting out discipline that is fair, and hopefully instructive. The teacher serves as a role model both by what they say and by what they do, inside and outside the classroom.

Maintain Appropriate Relationships with Students and Parents

Faculty members must also strive to convey respect, love, and concern for their students—and the students' parents—while not becoming too chummy with them. For some beginning teachers, it is a difficult distinction to make between being a teacher and a friend, but mistakes in this area can wreak untold havoc on classroom discipline and parent-teacher relationships. Overall teachers will wear many hats throughout a given day and solve many problems; all of these encounters provide a wonderful testing ground for administrative competencies.

Be Ready for Anything

School leaders, both administrators and faculty, must be able to think on their feet. Plenty of theorists posit solutions to every imaginable problem, but unfortunately, when a problem surfaces, there is usually little or no time to consult a recipe box for answers. Graduate programs often provide a few years for the educational leaders to study, reflect, and hone their dispositions.

Collegiality: Don't Start Teaching without It

Collegiality is an essential professional competency for educational leaders. It means that no one person has all the answers, and that truth and wisdom can be found in many persons. Collegiality also emphasizes a healthy interdependency among the members of a school community.

Graduate programs for educators can be a valuable resource here. The circle of friendships and professional expertise gained in these programs is extended and will serve as a network far beyond commencement and the conferral of a degree. Within a classroom setting with other professionals at similar career stages, graduate students are able to compare notes, discuss, and critique problems. This kind of setting is not dissimilar to a time when sisters would have gathered in the convent living room to prepare lesson plans together. Information is shared and—even more important—a sense of community develops.

Collegiality ultimately means having the skills and temperament to work with other people. Education is not the right field for anyone who lacks the capacity and ability to work with others. Educational leaders and all teachers who exemplify a collegial spirit generally have good self-knowledge; they know their talents as well as their shortcomings. Collegial leaders will not only enlist strengths that they lack from others but also defer to people who are equally proficient, or more gifted, and draw upon outside expertise. Robert Jones, the first lay principal at an elementary school on the West Coast where he has served for over thirty years, commented on the need for school leaders to have a collaborative disposition: "Especially in this day and age, leaders will be working with school boards and depending upon the wisdom of outside experts. Leaders will need help in making good decisions and should turn to the resources that are available."

Confidence for School Leaders

It is imperative to draw knowledgeable people into the support system of a parish school, but it is equally important for leaders to be confident in their background and talents to make good decisions and to lead the school. The Catholic Higher Education Supporting Catholic Schools programs that offer administrative degrees all strive to bolster the confidence that graduate students will need as academic, administrative, and spiritual leaders in their schools.

"Be true to yourself"—that is Principal Robert Jones's advice. Despite frequent visits to the former principal's new school to seek mentoring in his new role, he learned through the help of this sister principal that he had to learn to do things differently in ways that made sense for the current situation.

He felt that all new leaders will experience a brief honeymoon period during which school families will be pleased with the new vision and energy, but the problems are just waiting to step forward: "When the problems start coming along, about 50 percent of the people will love what you do, and 50 percent will not. This is why you have to be your own person, and people will respect you for that."

Much of school leadership centers on charting an overall vision of the school within the mission of the universal Church and local parish, and this vision is rooted in the knowledge of why the school exists and what it is trying to do. A principal will spend much of her or his time solving problems, and these are almost always connected to people.

Many leaders say that they spend about 90 percent of their time attending to about 10 percent of the organization's population. In dealing with the innumerable dilemmas or situations that arise on any given day, school leaders need a sense of confidence in their judgment; they should not wring their hands over what should be done. After all, this is why a leader is hired: to solve problems. Many bigger school questions need deliberation by a wider circle of expertise, but just as often there is a need to resolve situations immediately with only yourself as counsel.

Finding Confidence as a Spiritual Leader

There is probably no other area where this sense of confidence needs to be well grounded than in the realm of spiritual leadership. Knowledge of the Catholic faith and its educational philosophy as found in the many ecclesial documents is foundational for being a spiritual leader (see appendix B). The Catholic tradition will need to permeate the educational project at the school through the mission, academics, character and faith formation, and the manner in which people interact.

Sometimes it is difficult for lay educational leaders to see themselves as experts in Catholic matters, yet the students and families whom they serve will look to them to be well-educated resources conversant with the tradition, content, and current events of the Catholic Church. Some Catholic school professionals will begin this learning curve soon after they are hired as teachers, receive their religion textbook, and begin to delve into the topics that they will need to present in a convincing manner. At all levels of education, teachers will claim they learn more about a subject by teaching it than do the students. Because of this, many teachers will develop understanding on the job, and with each year of religion teaching that passes, these professionals will become more conversant in Catholicism.

School leaders will also find themselves dealing with many pastoral situations that require a sense of confidence: serious illness among the children and their families, the death of a child or parent, divorces, job loss, and so on. None of these matters can be totally outsourced to a pastor or religious sister.

Just as people have reasonable expectations that their doctors be knowledgeable about the latest procedure they saw on *Good Morning America*, so, too, will they look to Catholic school professionals to be familiar with some of the latest developments or trends in the Church. Teachers, especially, will field questions springing from the most recent news story, movie, television documentary, or popular YouTube video that touches on the Catholic faith. Some examples from popular culture are instructive.

When *The Da Vinci Code* was released in 2003, Catholics were plied with all kinds of ludicrous questions that often caught them off guard. This was a book that mixed facts and fiction, while purporting to be more history than fantasy. Television shows, other explanatory books, and an entire cottage industry were generated by the book and subsequent movie. Whatever one's personal opinion of the story, it was imperative for Catholic educators to be informed about the sensation. Similarly, Mel Gibson's *The Passion of the Christ* (2004) created a popular cultural phenomenon with critics both condemning and acclaiming the film.

Surely, these two cultural lightning rods sparked many discussions in Catholic schools and sent school leaders scurrying to grasp the questions and concerns about the content. These kinds of cultural realities will always come along, and wise professionals do not flee or shun an age-appropriate discussion with a class.

Cultural questions aside, Catholic school educators are regularly called on to provide spiritual leadership in liturgies. Many undergo catechetical formation when their class is asked to prepare a school liturgy; this can be a daunting task for someone who has only passively participated in Mass and has never served as an acolyte, gift bearer, lector, or choir member. Suddenly there is a hasty introduction to the church's lectionary, liturgical calendar, and missal.

Principals, pastors, and fellow faculty members should always be ready to assist the novice Mass planner, whose comfort level may fluctuate between sheer terror and mild panic at the prospect of planning and choreographing a Mass. Some have compared this experience to an attempt to perform open heart surgery when their only preparation was dissecting a frog in biology class. The People of God are very resilient, however, and even at times when a liturgy may fall short, everyone realizes that the planning is well intentioned. With time, confidence grows, as well as, one hopes, a sense of sound judgment and good taste.

All of these knowledge and competency areas are dynamic fields that need ongoing mastery. A good diocesan school office will offer excellent resources for continuing education in these areas. Continuous professional development should keep theorists and practitioners in fruitful communication.

Educators who have had access to scholarly or informed discussions are to be able to respond with knowledge, competence, and confidence to such topics. Today, information is abundant and easily accessible on the Internet, but it requires a judicious consumer to recognize reliable sources and to distinguish sound and reputable data from the cyber flotsam and jetsam.

Catholic Schools in the Future

For many years, the National Catholic Educational Association (NCEA) has been seeking to develop leadership for the schools. Working in tandem with this organization, CHESCS has responded to the need for Catholic school leadership by developing programs that prepare leaders. Many conferences of scholars have met over the years to discuss the future of Catholic education, and two such conferences deserve attention.

The two conferences of forty scholars from around the nation grew out of a discussion between Sister Lourdes Sheehan, RSM, then associate general secretary at the United States Conference of Catholic Bishops, and Sister Mary Peter Traviss, OP, director of the Institute of Catholic Educational Leadership at the University of San Francisco. The first conference in 2001 with the theme of "Catholic Educational Leaders Prepare for Their Successors: A Conversation" was held at the University of San Francisco. The topics included leadership, university and diocesan preparation programs, teacher recruitment and retention, and distance learning preparation.

This conference set the stage for a second conference in 2003 at the University of Dayton with the theme "Developing Educational Leadership: Continuing the Conversation." These two conferences developed recommendations around the following themes: essentials (what a Catholic leadership program must contain); the role of the principal (with special emphasis on survey research about this position); the disincentives to leadership (exploring what discourages competent candidates from pursuing leadership positions); the lay charism (investigating how the laity need to be supported); and outreach strategies (exploring ways to inform others about the conference and extend its work).

These pivotal and collegial meetings developed many recommendations for the leadership of the Church. Drawing upon this large body of work and expertise, a task force from the University of Notre Dame supplemented these proceedings in a response to the United States Conference of Catholic Bishops document *Renewing Our Commitment* (2005). This task force developed *Making God Known, Loved, and Served* (2008), a blueprint for the future. It addressed the four sections of *Renewing Our Commitment*, which are "[t]o strengthen Catholic identity, to attract and form talented leaders, to ensure academic excellence, and to finance Catholic schools so that they are accessible for all families."

The task force offered recommendations that many Catholic universities have had in place, but serve as good summary of how various sectors of the Church, especially Catholic universities, can assist. Among some of the more universally applicable points were the following recommendations:

1. Recruit and form a new generation of effective Catholic school teachers
2. Recruit and form effective Catholic school leaders
3. Cultivate a lay apostolic movement in service to Catholic schools

4. Build a national initiative for the academic improvement of Catholic schools
5. Build a national initiative to strengthen the Catholic identity of our schools
6. Form partnerships with other Catholic colleges and universities
7. Develop partnerships with individual Catholic schools
8. Attract and support the Latino community through our Catholic schools
9. Design and build consulting services to assist schools with management
10. Develop a national program for effective parish school leadership teams
11. Access public funds and resources for Catholic schools and their students[1]

The leadership of schools will continually need to be gauging the needs and direction of the Catholic school community, and most likely, in a few years, there will be other prescriptions for Catholic schools. As table 11.1 shows, although the number of Catholic schools has declined, they still remain an important part of the Catholic landscape.

Table 11.1. Catholic Schools in the United States (2011)

Diocesan, Parish, and Private	Number of Schools	Enrollment
Elementary schools	5,5858	1,517,708
Secondary schools	1,340	630, 587
TOTAL	5,7198	2,148,295

Educational Legacy Lives On

For those students who were taught by sisters, a unique educational experience was bestowed. It was a story of generosity and great courage in building a workforce that responded to the needs of a particular time. It is doubtful that the Church could have ever built the school system it did paying laity or the sisters a salary comparable to public school teachers. This generosity continues to be mirrored in the laymen and laywomen who have succeeded the sisters.

Financing the schools has always been a major struggle and will remain so in the United States. One of the major challenges for all Catholic elementary schools is that tuition can only be raised so high, and many poor and middle-class families will not have the ability, even with assistance, to provide a Catholic education for their children.

It is unlikely and unwise to presume that a workforce such as the sisters will come to the rescue in number or quality.

However, certainly volunteer groups of teachers, like the PLACE Corps and ACE, are great mirrors of the zeal that the sisters brought to bear. Ongoing education programs and partnerships between Catholic higher education and dioceses are also helping form competent and confident leaders for the schools, and professional development degrees enhance the quality of Catholic education and ensure the ongoing progress of schools founded by sisters.

Communities of sisters with long-standing histories in elementary education might consider developing programs like that of the Sisters of St. Joseph of Orange with their CSJ Educational Network. Every community has wisdom and experience from which new leaders can benefit. Communities can continue to develop ways of being present to Catholic schools.

Along with providing these new lay leaders with the knowledge, competencies, and confidence to be excellent academic and spiritual leaders, there is a need to assist the clergy. New York Archbishop Timothy Dolan has called for a re-evangelization of the clergy toward Catholic schools. Bishops should strive to place no pastor in a parish with a school unless he completely supports it. Seminary programs and continuing education programs for pastors could explore ways to promote the value of Catholic schools more effectively among seminarians and priests.

While the number of sisters continues to level off, there are encouraging statistics about rising interest in religious life and increased vocations among communities with a teaching charism. Perhaps the torch passes from one community to another when a mission is accomplished. In the case of communities that are growing, as well as those that are declining, there remains a call for prayers and the gratitude of a nation.

When one reviews the history of Catholic elementary schools in the United States, it is impossible to see any growth, development, or achievement without the labors of religious sisters. John Patrick Shanley dedicated *Doubt*, his 2005 Pulitzer Prize–winning play and 2005 Best Play of the Year, to religious sisters with these words: "The play is dedicated to the many orders of Catholic nuns who devoted their lives to serving others in hospitals, schools, and retirement homes. Though they have been much maligned and ridiculed, who among us has been so generous?"

Perhaps second only to the power of the Trinity, the saints, and the sacraments, when it comes to human efforts contributing to the growth of Catholicism in the United States, no achievement will ever parallel the love and labors of the sisters.

~

Postscript

Each year, during the second week of Advent, every parish in the United States takes up a collection for retired religious to help provide for their living expenses and rising health-care costs. These funds are distributed among the numerous religious communities that invested all their resources into the service of building up the Church and literally gave everything for the education and welfare of generations. Learn more at www.retiredreligious.org.

~

Appendix A

St. Louis Convent
117 Ong Street
El Monte, California
27 August 1949

My dear Mothers and Sisters:

You will all be eager to get news of our arrival and of the beginnings of our work in America. The few hurried notes I was able to send along the journey were of necessity very brief. At New York we were met on board the Queen Elizabeth by Mr. O'Brien and Mr. Gillen, representatives of Mayor O'Dwyer. Fr. Shanley, whom Mr. deValera had asked to meet us, was also there, and Mr. Connolly of the Irish Echo. He had made the coming of the St. Louis nuns front page news in the Echo and had organized a reception committee. Being sponsored by the Mayor obtained our speedy exit through the customs. Some of the Officers who hailed from Monaghan were very glad to see us and anxious to do everything in their power to assist us. As we waited, the Sisters' relatives and other friends of the Congregation, past pupils and others, came forward. Maurice Leahey, an old friend, was also there.

When formalities were completed, we set out for the City Hall in cars provided by the Mayor, Fr. Shanley, and Mr. Connolly. Friends of the Sisters were invited to attend also, all very proud to welcome the St. Louis Sisters to America. The

Mayor received us very graciously at the City Hall, Fr. Shanley introducing us. He shook hands with all present and in a very happy speech, welcomed the St. Louis nuns to America, after which he sat with us for a photograph.

We then set out for the Convent of the Sacred Heart of Mary, where Sr. M. Darerea's sister, Madam Fidelma, had invited us. The Mother Superior received us very kindly and brought us to our rooms. This is a very beautiful Convent and we were very comfortable. After we got some rest and refreshments, Mr. Connolly and Mr. Cowan came back to take us out to see the City. We first visited St. Patrick's Cathedral, the most beautiful Church any of us had ever seen. We were especially delighted to find a Statue of St. Louis there. We drove through Harlem, saw the Empire State Building, Fordham University, and ended it at a new school of the Sisters of the Sacred Heart of Mary, Marymount. This school is on a magnificently elegant scale, the Sisters told us that they will be in debt for another generation to pay for it. Mr. Connolly took us back to the Convent via Broadway, to see the lights. On our return to the Convent a sumptuous dinner awaited us and the Sisters showered attention on us. Madam Peter Elliott, a past pupil of Kilkeel, was especially pleased to see us, and Madame Fidelma had particular charge of us. People who could not come to the reception called us on the telephone, regretting our hurried departure from New York. We were rather relieved to get off early the next morning, after Holy Mass.

At the Grand Central Station we had Cook's representatives to look after our luggage and help us generally. Maurice Leahey gave us candles and his book on Nano Nagle. The train left at 8:00 o'clock for Dunkirk, the nearest station to Silver Creek. The scenery along the banks of the Hudson was beautiful, but we were tired and slept for part of the journey. Frs. Paul and Joseph Connellee and Fr. Loftus met us at the Dunkirk at 7:00 P.M. and drove us out to Silver Creek, where a truly Irish welcome awaited us from the Columban Sisters. Mother Mary Brendan and her Community really overwhelmed us with kindness. We spent two very happy days at Silver Creek. On Saturday morning, the Rector, Fr. Connellee offered Holy Mass for all our intentions. After breakfast he showed us over to the Seminary, which is only a little distance from the Convent. We had some delightful walks along the shore of Lake Erie. A group of Mercy Sisters from Buffalo were holidaying in the huts, which formed the original Silver Creek Seminary. They come here every summer and enjoy a very happy holiday. One of the Columban Fathers acts as their Chaplain. Fr. Lenahan, who was a prisoner of the Reds in China, gave Benediction in the evening and afterwards stayed to see us. He gave us very interesting details of the Mexican Mission in Los Angeles, where he worked for some time.

A very enjoyable part of our visit was our recreations with the Sisters. It did us good to see them so gay and simple, and so very, very kind to us. Mother Mary Brendan left nothing undone to make us feel at home and gave us huge parcels of provisions for our journey. We left at 9:00 P.M. on Sunday night in three cars driven by the Fathers to Dunkirk.

Here began our first experience of sleeping in the train. Dressing and undressing in bed was the most difficult part of it. The black porter was quite concerned when he found that Sr. M. Killian had reached the top bunk without a ladder. He reproved her gently and said she might hurt herself if she did it again. The ladder was used after that.

We arrived about 7:30 A.M. in Chicago on Monday morning, the Feast of Immaculate Heart. Fr. Murphy, St. Gertrude's Rectory, met us with a car; and Mr. & Mrs. Finnegan, Sr. M. Hildegarde's cousins, were also there. We drove to the Cathedral for Mass and Holy Communion. A sung Mass was going on and two other Masses at side Altars. We were very happy to finish our Novena to the Immaculate Heart, with Holy Mass, after which we went to Mundelein College, a huge establishment run by the Sisters of Charity of the Sacred Heart. Fr. Murphy, to whom the Balla Sisters introduced us, teaches Religion in the College. Here again we were very hospitably received and served to a delicious breakfast. Sr. M. Columba Kelly from Dublin paid us particular attention. We were shown through the college and were lost in admiration at all the splendor. It is a seven story building, with every possible up to date equipment. One floor is given over entirely to music, harmony and orchestra rooms, music rooms with a grand piano each, music library, etc. Science, Biology, Physics, and Chemistry Laboratories were all on a grand scale too. Another floor was given over to Home Economics, or, as we could call it, "Domestic Economy." When we reached the swimming pool we found the door locked, and Sister explained that some of the Sisters were having a swim. We thought that Cardinal Mundelein had built this college, but Sr. Columba explained that he just gave it his blessing and his name—no cash! Nearby is Loyola University. We visited the church dedicated to Our Lady Della Strada. There were beautiful paintings of the Jesuit Martyrs, stained glass windows donated by the Kellys, Murphys, Kilgallons, and other familiar names.

Fr. Murphy and a friend, Patricia Finn, drove us in two cars, first to St. Gertrude's church, which is very beautiful. We then set out for Mundelein Seminary, the largest in the world. It is here the Secular Priests of the Diocese of Chicago are educated. Cardinal Mundelein built and endowed it. We saw the autographed photograph of Pius XII, presented by him when he visited the Eucharistic Congress in Chicago, as Cardinal Pacelli. There is a Benedictine Convent with Perpetual Adoration at some distance from the Seminary. This was founded by Cardinal Mudelein, to pray for students. The Chapel is very magnificent, two Sisters were in adoration.

We returned to Chicago and had dinner with Mr. and Mrs. Finnegan, after which we visited the Mother Cabrini Hospital and said our Rosary in public in her room. The Sister on duty gave us souvenirs. The bed Mother Cabrini died in is there, her chair, and the Statue of Our Lady that she carried everywhere with her, and also a Statue of the Holy Child.

Fr. Murphy, Mr. and Mrs. Finnegan saw us to the train at 9:00 P.M. We slept very well, arriving next morning in Omaha at 8:00 A.M. Fr. Kielt, the Rector, and Fr. Hanahoe met us at the station and drove us to the Seminary. A Priest was waiting to say Mass and we received Holy Communion. After breakfast, the Fathers entertained us, showed us the grounds. There is a beautiful grotto here and an unusual Statue of St. Columban. After dinner, prayers, and a rest, Frs. Brennan and Hanahoe drove us to visit Boys Town, some distance outside Omaha. Boys Town covers a huge area, the Church is magnificent. There are Trade Schools, Carpentry, Printing, Modeling, and an immense Stadium, in which we watched a game of baseball. A monument erected to the memory of Monsignor Flanagan reminded one of St. John Bosco. The boys were wandering around, some cycling; others going bathing; some came over and said, "Hello, Sisters." We watched a young boy modeling a Statue of Our Lady. They make all kinds of souvenirs and sell them in a souvenir shop. One of the teachers in the modeling school had been in Ireland during the war, in Londonderry and Enniskillen. Monsignor Flanagan's last idea was to house the boys in cottages, about 25 in each, so as to give them some idea of home life.

We returned to St. Columbans at 6:00 P.M. for supper, after which Fr. Brennan showed us a film of Missionary work in Japan. We met Fr. McElroy here. He was interested in various items of Clogher news. Fr. Tim Connelly was absent, much to our regret. Monsignor McPolin and the other Fathers were really more than kind to us. They drove us to the train at 9:30 P.M.

Again we went to bed, by now quite used to sleeping on the train. Next day, Wednesday, and that night passed pleasantly enough. The black attendants on the train were very attentive to all our wants, but the meals on the dining car were a fabulous price. Luckily we had only one day to provide for.

Before leaving Omaha, Fr. Kevin McNally telephoned that Fr. Ginty and he would meet us at Pomona, thus saving us an hour's train time to Los Angeles. We were glad when the train stopped at 10:00 A.M., a special stop being made at Pomona, so that the Sisters could alight. Fr. Ginty and his Assistant, Fr. Faughan, Fr. McNally and his camera awaited us on the platform and some ladies of the Parish. We drove to the convent, where Fr. John Conlan and Sister Mary Madeline's brother, Fr. John Joe Healy, S.J. received us. Fr. Healy got special permission to wait over to greet us. Fr. Ginty celebrated Holy Mass and we received Holy Communion. The other Priest had Mass with us in the Oratory. We were happy to begin our first American Foundation on St. Louis Day. Mrs. Baumgartner, President of the Ladies Catholic Society in the Parish, prepared breakfast and had everything in readiness. Breakfast at half past eleven was very welcome, even though the tea was not up to Irish standards. Since then the quality of the tea has improved. After breakfast, Fr. Ginty brought us through the Convent, which is really very spacious, and, to our ideas, luxurious. The ground floor is of oak blocks, upstairs some kind of rubber. There are nine cells, a store room, linen store, bathrooms and toilets upstairs. On the ground floor two large rooms, separated by folding doors, one the Community Room, and the other the Refectory. Continuous with these are a Pantry, Kitchen, and Laundry. The kitchen has a large gas stove, with a special light and electrically worked clock. A very large refrigerator, and all cooking utensils and equipment are better than anything we have ever seen.

The Laundry has a Thor Washing machine and Wringer, which is operated by electricity. The Sisters have used these to good advantage already.

The Chapel is simple and beautiful. The oak Altar is Liturgical, with six tall candlesticks and two small ones, a beautiful bronze cylindrical Tabernacle, surmounted by a Dove. The photographs will describe all this later. Each Sister has a Prieu Dieu and chair. The Sacristy is furnished and stocked with everything necessary.

Monsignor McNicholas, whose parents come from Mayo, is our Ordinary Confessor. He came today and like all the Priests we have met, is genuinely delighted to welcome the St. Louis Nuns to America. He gave us some good advice in the Parlor. Among other things, that we must never say that "we don't know." That would be fatal. Our way is "the way."

To return to St. Louis Day—Monsignor Dignan, the Supervisor of Schools, called to welcome us, and to assure us of his guidance and help, in any difficulty.

Telegrams and letters awaited us from the Houses in Ireland, England, and Africa, and from friends in America. Bishop Manning's telegram reads:

"YOU ARE MOST WELCOME TO CALIFORNIA. MAY ST. LOUIS SMILE A BLESSING ON YOU THIS DAY."

Bishop McGouken wired:

"MAY THE ANGELS GUARD YOU AND YOUR COMMUNITY AND MAKE YOU HAPPY HERE."

At 4:00 o'clock, Fr. Ginty, Fr. Faughan, and Fr. Kevin McNealy drove us out to Westminster to the Columban Sisters Convent. Mother Mary Therese had very kindly invited us for our St. Louis Day dinner. Fr. John O'Daly, who had been giving the Retreat, gave us a great welcome. We had a very pleasant evening with the Sisters. After Benediction we set out for "HOME." Fr. Ginty's car had a radio and the program included "MY LAGAN LOVE," and "THE DONOVANS." "THE TOP OF THE MORNING"—that's how the Irish say "Hello." To our surprise we found the back of the car well filled with provisions, very thoughtfully bestowed by Mother Mary Therese—brown bread, fruit, sugar, tea, preserves, etc.

A huge box of beautiful flowers and a note of welcome were sent by Mother Mary Francis of the Holy Child Sisters, Pasadena. She had heard from Mother Hilegarde that we were coming and wrote offering her assistance in any way she could help.

The day ended with the Rosary, followed by the Magnificat in thanksgiving for our safe arrival in California, and the Hymn to St. Louis. We had the Rosary in common every day since we left Ireland, and by a strange coincidence when the train stopped at Salt Lake City—the City of the Mormons—we were saying the Rosary. We had Mass every day on our journey, except the morning of our arrival in London and one morning in the train.

Hilton, the janitor, the Mr. Cullen of El Monte, made a Pedestal for the Statue of Our Lady of Fatima, which arrived intact, and now adorns our Little Oratory.

Preparations for school have started already. Fr. Ginty took the Sisters through the school and initiated them into the mysteries of files and forms, card indexes, transfers, achievement charts, registration cards, etc. The subjects are: Religion, Computation, Problems, Grammar, Languages, History, Geography, Spelling,

Vocabulary, Reading. It all sounds very formidable and complicated, but of course we mustn't say, "We don't know."

Fr. Tom McEnnis is here visiting Sr. Mary Claudine. He has a commission from his Bishop to secure a St. Louis Community for his Parish in Seattle. He has given us some useful hints. He is a very zealous young priest and rejoices that we have such a grand opportunity of doing much needed work for souls here.

Today, Sunday, we heard Holy Mass with the parishioners in the School Auditorium, which is being used as a church. There were big congregations at the 7:00 and 9:00 o'clock Masses, and there were three other Masses as well. Today, there is to be a reception for the Sisters from 1:00 till 3:00, just to meet the people. Fr. Ginty is very anxious that we shall have all we need. He is a kindly, gentle priest, and seems to be a very hard worker.

It is a new parish and a poor one. Announcements were made at the Masses about the sale of tickets—the money raising effort for this year.

This is just an outline of events up to date. The Sisters are very well and cheerful. The heat is intense, but the nights are cool—even cold. The kindness of the Columban priest and Sisters made the long trans-continental journey much easier. We can never forget their hospitality and readiness to take great trouble to entertain us. We felt we were reaping the fruits of the prayers offered all over the Congregation for this new Foundation. We have much to thank God for, and much to ask Him for. Let us all by our charity, generosity, and fervent prayers try to win for the Congregation every grace and blessing needful for all its works. Pray especially for many more vocations.

Mother Mary Ronan and the Sisters join me in sending loving wishes to all our Mothers and Sisters everywhere. Now more than ever do we need to live and think and pray "that we may be one." God bless you all.

Your Loving in J.C.,
M. Columbanus

~

Appendix B

Church Documents on Catholic Education

The Vatican

Leo XIII. (1879). *Aeterni Patris: On Restoring Christian Philosophy.*
Leo XIII. (November 27, 1885). *Spectata Fides: On Christian Education.*
Leo XIII. (1889). *Magni Nobis: On the Catholic University of America.*
Pius XI. (1929). *Rappresentanti in Terra: On Christian Education.*
Pius XI. (December 31, 1929). *Divini Illius Magistri: On Christian Education.*
Sacred Congregation for Catholic Education. (1977). *The Catholic School.*
John Paul II. (1979). *Sapientia Christiana: On Ecclesiastical Universities.*
Sacred Congregation for Catholic Education. (1982). *Lay Catholics in Schools: Witness to Faith.*
Sacred Congregation for Catholic Education. (1983). *Educational Guidance in Human Love.*
Flannery, A. (1988). *Documents of the Second Vatican Council. Gravissimum Educationis: Declaration on Education.*
Sacred Congregation for Catholic Education. (1988). *The Religious Dimension of the Education in a Catholic School.*
John Paul II. (1990). *Ex Corde Ecclesiae: On Catholic Universities.*
Sacred Congregation for Catholic Education. (June 7, 1994). *The Presence of the Church in the University and in University Culture.*
Sacred Congregation for Catholic Education. (December 28, 1997). *The Catholic School on the Verge of the Third Millennium.*
Sacred Congregation for Catholic Education. (November 20, 2002). *Consecrated Persons and Their Mission in Schools.*

United States Conference of Catholic Bishops

USCCB (1972). *To Teach as Jesus Did.*

USCCB (1985). *Empowered by the Spirit: Campus Ministry Faces the Future.*

USCCB (1990). *In Support of Catholic Elementary and Secondary Schools.*

USCCB (1998). *Sharing Catholic Social Teaching: Challenges and Directions.*

USCCB (1998). *Welcome and Justice for Persons with Disabilities.*

USCCB (1999). *Sharing Catholic Social Teaching: Challenges and Directions.*

USCCB (1999). *Faithful Citizenship: Political Responsibility for a New Millennium.*

USCCB (1999). *Our Hearts Were Burning within Us: A Pastoral Plan for Adult Faith Formation in the United States.*

USCCB (2000). *The Application of Ex Corde Ecclesiae for the United States.*

USCCB (2001). *Guidelines Concerning the Academic Mandatum in Catholic Universities (Canon 812).*

USCCB (2005). *Renewing Our Commitment to Catholic Elementary and Secondary Schools in the Third Millennium.*

Endnotes

Chapter 1: What Led to the Massive Catholic School System?

1. Catherine Kealey and Robert Kealey, *On Their Shoulders: A Short Biographical History of American Catholic Schools* (Washington, DC: NCEA, 2003), 390.

2. G. P. Moran, *Sending Out Ireland's Poor: Assisted Emigration to North America in the Nineteenth Century* (Portland, OR: Four Courts Press, 2004).

3. Jay P. Dolan, *The American Catholic Experiment* (New York: Galilee Books, 1985), 128.

4. Diane Ravitch, *The Great School Wars: New York City, 1805–1973* (Baltimore: Johns Hopkins University Press, 1988), 5–6.

5. Ravitch, *The Great School Wars: New York City*, 36.

6. This inflammatory nickname is more popularly associated with his fiery temper and passion for his flock. However, the reality is not quite as exciting as the myth; when a bishop signs his name on a document, it is preceded by the symbol of the Holy Cross. Hence, Archbishop Hughes's signature cross resembled a dagger, and given his pugnacious temperament, that may have been intentional.

7. John J. Hennesey, *American Catholics* (Oxford: Oxford University Press, 1983), 124.

8. Hennesey, *American Catholics*, 173.

9. Hennesey, *American Catholics*, 174.

10. J. P. Dolan, *In Search of an American Catholicism: A History of Religion and Culture in Tension* (Oxford: Oxford University Press, 2002), 60.

11. Martin E. Marty, *A Short History of American Catholicism* (Allen, TX: Thomas More, 1995), 140.

12. Thomas C. Hunt, Thomas Oldenski, and Theodore J. Wallace, *Catholic School Leadership: An Invitation to Lead* (London: Falmer Press, 2000), 40.

13. Suellen M. Hoy, *Good Hearts: Catholic Sisters in Chicago's Past* (Chicago: University of Illinois Press, 2006), 93.

14. "Ulysses S. Grant," *Encyclopaedia Britannica's Guide to American Presidents* (2008), www.britannica.com/presidents/article-9116880, accessed August 11, 2008.

15. Y. Hart, "Blaine Amendment," in *Catholic Schools in the United States: An Encyclopedia*, Vol. 1 (Westport, CT: Greenwood Press, 2004), 71–72.

16. M. C. Klinkhamer, "Blaine Amendment," in *New Catholic Encyclopedia*, Vol. 2 (Washington, DC: Catholic University of America Press, 1967), 598.

Chapter 2: Finding the Sisters

1. Doug Owram, *Born at the Right Time: A History of the Baby Boom Generation* (Toronto: University of Toronto Press, 1997).

2. Dolan, *The American Catholic Experiment*, 287.

3. Francis J. Weber, *His Eminence of Los Angeles: James Francis Cardinal McIntyre* (Mission Hills, CA: Saint Francis Historical Society, 1997), 249.

4. Weber, *His Eminence of Los Angeles*, 284.

5. Anita Marie Caspary, *Witness to Integrity: The Crisis of the Immaculate Heart Community of California* (Collegeville, MN: Liturgical Press, 2003).

6. All of the correspondence between the Archdiocese of Los Angeles and the Sisters of St. Louis is from the archives of the Sisters of St. Louis (reprinted with permission of the Roman Catholic Archbishop of Los Angeles, a corporation sole, and its affiliated entities).

Chapter 3: Preparing the Sisters for Teaching, Making Sacrifices

1. Ann Carey, *Sisters in Crisis: The Tragic Unraveling of Women's Religious Communities* (Huntington, IN: Our Sunday Visitor Publishing Division, 1997), 134.

2. Kevina Keating, CCVI, and Mary Peter Traviss, OP, *Pioneer Mentoring in Teacher Preparation* (St. Cloud, MN: North Star Press, 2001), 93–94.

3. Keating and Traviss, *Pioneer Mentoring in Teacher Preparation*, 75.

Chapter 4: From the Motherhouse to the Classroom

1. Keating, CCVI, and Traviss, OP, *Pioneer Mentoring in Teacher Preparation*, 34.

2. Thomas Sergiovanni, *Leadership for the Schoolhouse* (San Francisco: Jossey-Bass, 1996).

3. See www.ascjus.org/us-province/index.aspx.

4. L. C. De Beuckelaer, "Sisters of Charity of Leavenworth (SCL)," in *New Catholic Encyclopedia*, Vol. 3 (New York: McGraw-Hill: New York, 1967), 475–76.

5. De Beuckelaer, "Sisters of Charity of Leavenworth."

Chapter 5: Working with Pastors

1. Dolan, *The American Catholic Experiment*, 277.
2. Andrew Greeley, *Priests: A Calling in Crisis* (Chicago: University of Chicago Press, 2005).
3. Tracy Schier and Cynthia Russett, *Catholic Women's Colleges in America* (Baltimore: Johns Hopkins University Press, 2002).
4. Dolan, *The American Catholic Experiment*, 289.

Chapter 6: Changes in Religious Life Lead to Departures

1. The 2009 CARA vocation study *Recent Vocations to Religious Life: A Report for the National Religious Vocation Conference* and related information is available at www.nrvc.net.
2. John Allen Jr., "More Snippets from a Conversation with Mother Millea," *National Catholic Reporter*, February 23, 2010.
3. Carey, *Sisters in Crisis*, 317.
4. J. Hickey, *Origins* (Washington, DC: Catholic News Service, March 23, 1989), 691–92.
5. Carey, *Sisters in Crisis*, 33–34.
6. John Fialka, *Sisters: Catholic Nuns and the Making of America* (New York: St. Martin's Griffin, 2003), 212.

Chapter 7: The Sisters Reflect upon Their Experiences

1. G. W. Bush, 2008 State of the Union Address, United States Congress, www.voanews.com/english/news/a-13-2008-01-29-voa6-66596442.html.
2. *Recent Vocations to Religious Life* (2009).
3. Elise Jones and Charles F. Westoff, "The End of 'Catholic' Fertility," *Demography*, May 16, 1979.
4. More information about the Spiritual Exercises of St. Ignatius can be found at www.ignatianspirituality.com.
5. J. H. Newman, *An Essay on the Development of Christian Doctrine* (New York: Doubleday, 1960).

Chapter 8: When a School Closed

1. "Domincan Sisters Bid Farewell," *Catholic Sentinel*, June 22, 2007.
2. "Domincan Sisters Bid Farewell," *Catholic Sentinel*, June 22, 2007.
3. Michael Garanzini, "Dealing with Narcissistic Families: Lessons for Educational Leadership in Parent and Child Guidance," in *Catholic School Leadership: An Invitation to Lead*, edited by Thomas C. Hunt, Thomas Oldenski, and Theodore J. Wallace (New York: Falmer Press, 2000), 244–58.

4. M. P. Caruso, "Social Capital," in *Catholic Schools in the United States: An Encyclopedia*, Vol. 2 (Westport, CT: Greenwood Press, 2004), 608.

Chapter 9: Lay Leadership Emerges

1. *Lay Catholics in Schools: Witnesses to Faith* (1982), #16.
2. U.S. Conference of Catholic Bishops, *Renewing Our Commitment to Catholic Elementary and Secondary Schools in the Third Millennium* (Washington, DC: U.S. Conference of Catholic Bishops, 2005), 10–11.
3. Kealey and Kealey, *On Their Shoulders*, 109.
4. Jack Star, "Trouble Ahead for the Catholic Schools," *Look* 27, no. 21 (1963): 37–40.
5. Star, "Trouble Ahead," 37.
6. Star, "Trouble Ahead," 38.
7. Star, "Trouble Ahead."
8. Carol Lynn, personal communication, April 7, 2008.

Chapter 10: Transition and Signs of Renewal

1. Suellen M. Hoy, *Good Hearts: Catholic Sisters in Chicago's Past* (Chicago: University of Illinois Press, 2006), 1.
2. Diana Murphy, personal communication (March 17, 2008).
3. Austin Flannery, ed., *Vatican Council II: The Conciliar and Post Conciliar Documents* (Dublin: Dominican Publication, 1975).
4. Father Thomas Sherman, SJ, personal communication (April 10, 2007).

Chapter 11: The Future of Catholic Schools and the Legacy of the Sisters

1. Notre Dame Task Force on Catholic Education, *Making God Known, Loved, and Served: The Future of Catholic Primary and Secondary Schools in the United States* (2008), available at http://ace.nd.edu/files/task_force_report.pdf.

~

Bibliography

Allen, John, Jr. "More Snippets from a Conversation with Mother Millea." *National Catholic Reporter*, February 23, 2010.

Belluck, P. "Catholic Lay Group Tests a Strategy Change." *New York Times*, June 24, 2007. http://www.nytimes.com/2007/06/24/us/24voice.html?_r=1.

Bennett, M. J. *When Dreams Came True: The GI Bill and the Making of Modern America*. Washington, DC: Brassey's, 1996.

Bippus, S. "The Whining Center." *School* 65, no. 9 (2008): 50.

Bolman, L., and T. Deal. *Reframing Organizations: Artistry, Choice, and Leadership*. 3rd ed. San Francisco: Jossey-Bass, 2003.

Buetow, H. A. *The Catholic School: Its Roots, Identity, and Future*. New York: Crossroad, 1988.

———. *Of Singular Benefit: The Story of Catholic Education in the United States*. New York: Macmillan, 1970.

Bush, G. W. 2008 State of the Union Address. United States Congress. www.voanews.com/english/news/a-13-2008-01-29-voa6-66596442.html.

Carey, Ann. *Sisters in Crisis: The Tragic Unraveling of Women's Religious Communities*. Huntington, IN: Our Sunday Visitor Publishing Division, 1997.

Carty, T. J. *A Catholic in the White House? Religion, Politics, and John F. Kennedy's Presidential Campaign*. New York: Palgrave Macmillan, 2004.

Caruso, M. P. "Cristo Rey Schools." In *Catholic Schools in the United States: An Encyclopedia*, Vol. 1 (197–98). Westport, CT: Greenwood Press, 2004.

———. "Future Shepherds and Catholic Elementary Schools." *Seminary Journal* 10, no. 1 (2004): 68–73.

———. "Social Capital." In *Catholic Schools in the United States: An Encyclopedia*, Vol. 2 (608–9). Westport, CT: Greenwood Press, 2004.

Caspary, Anita Marie. *Witness to Integrity: The Crisis of the Immaculate Heart Community of California.* Collegeville, MN: Liturgical Press, 2003.

Coleman, J. *Foundations of Social Theory.* Cambridge, MA: Belknap Press, 1998.

Day, T. *Why Catholics Can't Sing: The Culture of Catholicism and the Triumph of Bad Taste.* New York: Crossroad, 1990.

De Beuckelaer, L. C. "Sisters of Charity of Leavenworth (SCL)." In *New Catholic Encyclopedia,* Vol. 3 (475–76). New York: McGraw-Hill, 1967.

Dolan, Jay P. *The American Catholic Experiment.* New York: Galilee Books, 1985.

———. *In Search of an American Catholicism: A History of Religion and Culture in Tension.* Oxford: Oxford University Press, 2002.

"Dominican Sisters Bid Farewell." *Catholic Sentinel,* February 26, 2008. http://www.sentinel.org/node/8169.

Ellis, J. T. *American Catholicism.* 2nd ed. Chicago: University of Chicago Press, 1969.

Ewens, M. "Women in the Convent." In *American Catholic Women,* edited by K. Kennelly. New York: Macmillan, 1989.

Fessenden, F. "Changes in the Catholic Church, Changes in Its Flock." *New York Times,* April 19, 2008. http://query.nytimes.com/gst/fullpage.html?res=9903E5DA1130F93AA25757C0A96E9C8B63&sec=&spon=&pagewanted=print.

Fialka, John. *Sisters: Catholic Nuns and the Making of America.* New York: St. Martin's Griffin, 2003.

Flannery, Austin, ed. *Vatican Council II: The Conciliar and Post Conciliar Documents.* Dublin: Dominican Publication, 1975.

Fullan, M. *Leading in a Culture of Change.* San Francisco: Jossey-Bass, 2003.

Garanzini, M. "Dealing with Narcissistic Families: Lessons for Educational Leadership in Parent and Child Guidance." In *Catholic School Leadership: An Invitation to Lead,* edited by Thomas C. Hunt, Thomas Oldenski, and Theodore J. Wallace. New York: Falmer Press, 2000.

Greeley, Andrew. *Priests: A Calling in Crisis.* Chicago: University of Chicago Press, 2005.

———. "Signs of Life." *Commonweal* 135. August 15, 2008.

———. "The So-Called Failure of Catholic Schools." *Phi Delta Kappan* 80, no. 1 (1998): 24–25.

———. "The Treason of the Clerks: Church Leaders and Catholic Educators Are Killing Catholic Schools." *National Catholic Reporter,* April 8, 2005.

Greeley, A., William McCready, and Kathleen McCourt. *Catholic Schools in a Declining Church.* Kansas City: Sheed & Ward, 1976.

Greeley, A., and Peter G. Rossi. *The Education of Catholic Americans.* Chicago: Aldine, 1966.

Greene, R. *The 48 Laws of Power.* New York: Penguin, 1998.

Hart, Y. "Blaine Amendment." In *Catholic Schools in the United States: An Encyclopedia,* Vol. 1 (71–72). Westport, CT: Greenwood Press, 2004.

Henderson, N., and Mike M. Milstein. *Resiliency in Schools: Making It Happen for Students and Educators.* Updated edition. Thousand Oaks, CA: Corwin Press, 2002.

Hennesey, John J. *American Catholics.* Oxford: Oxford University Press, 1983.

Hickey, J. *Origins.* Washington, DC: Catholic News Service, March 23, 1989.

Hoy, Suellen M. *Good Hearts: Catholic Sisters in Chicago's Past.* Chicago: University of Illinois Press, 2006.

Hunt, Thomas C. "The History of Catholic Schools in the United States: An Overview." In *Catholic School Leadership: An Invitation to Lead,* edited by Thomas C. Hunt, Thomas Oldenski, and Theodore J. Wallace. New York: Falmer Press, 2000.

Hunt, Thomas C., Ellis A. Joseph, and Ronald J. Nuzzi, eds. *Catholic Schools in the United States: An Encyclopedia.* Volume 1. Westport, CT: Greenwood Press, 2004.

Hunt, Thomas C., Thomas Oldenski, and Theodore J. Wallace. *Catholic School Leadership: An Invitation to Lead.* London: Falmer Press, 2000.

Ignatian Spirituality. April 21, 2008. www.bc.edu/bc_org/prs/stign/ignatian_spirit.html.

John Paul II. *Apostolic Constitution Ex Corde Ecclesiae of the Supreme Pontiff John Paul II on Catholic Universities.* Boston: St. Paul Books and Media, 1990.

Jones, Elise, and Charles F. Westoff. "The End of 'Catholic' Fertility." *Demography,* May 16, 1979.

Kealey, Catherine, and Robert Kealey. *On Their Shoulders: A Short Biographical History of American Catholic Schools.* Washington, DC: NCEA, 2003.

Keating, Kevina, CCVI, and Mary Peter Traviss, OP. *Pioneer Mentoring in Teacher Preparation.* St. Cloud, MN: North Star Press, 2001.

Klinkhamer, M. C. "Blaine Amendment." In *New Catholic Encyclopedia.* Volume 2. Washington, DC: Catholic University of America Press, 1967.

Kübler-Ross, E. *On Death and Dying.* New York: Macmillan, 1969.

Lay Catholics in Schools: Witnesses to Faith. The Sacred Congregation for Catholic Education. Vatican City, October 15, 1982. Accessed March 10, 2008. www.vatican.va/roman_curia/congregations/ccatheduc/documents/rc_con_ccatheduc_doc_19821015_lay-catholics_en.html.

Leigh, P. R. "Segregation by Gerrymander: The Creation of the Lincoln Heights (Ohio) School District." *Journal of Negro Education* 66, no. 2 (1997): 121–36.

Lovely, S. *Principalship: Finding, Coaching, and Mentoring School Leaders* (2004). March 31, 2009. http://linus.lmu.edu/search~S1?/.b1488230/.b1488230/1,1,1,B/l856~b1488230&FF=&1,0,,1,0.

Lum, L. "Handling 'Helicopter Parents.'" *Diverse: Issues in Higher Education* 23, no. 20 (November 2006): 40–43.

Marty, Martin E. *A Short History of American Catholicism.* Allen, TX: Thomas More, 1995.

Massa, M. *Anti-Catholicism in America: The Last Acceptable Prejudice.* New York: Crossroad, 2003.

Moran, G. P. *Sending Out Ireland's Poor: Assisted Emigration to North America in the Nineteenth Century.* Portland, OR: Four Courts Press, 2004.

Newman, J. H. *An Essay on the Development of Christian Doctrine.* New York: Doubleday, 1960.

Notre Dame Task Force on Catholic Education. *Making God Known, Loved, and Served: The Future of Catholic Primary and Secondary Schools in the United States.* 2008. Available at http://ace.nd.edu/assets/2296/tf_cover.pdf.

Official Catholic Directory. New Providence, NJ: P. J. Kenedy and Sons, 2011.

Owram, Doug. *Born at the Right Time: A History of the Baby Boom Generation.* Toronto: University of Toronto Press, 1997.

Pius XII. *Counsel to Teaching Sisters. An Address by His Holiness Pope Pius XII Given September 15, 1951 to the First International Congress of Teaching Sisters.* www.papalencyclicals.net/Pius12/P12TCHRS.HTM.

Price, C. "Closing with Pride . . . and Moving to the Future: 91-Year-Old School Exits Graciously and Gratefully." *Momentum: The Official Journal of the National Catholic Educational Association* 39, no. 1 (2008): 28–29.

Quinn, Sr. Edward William, IHM. *It's a Catholic School: Let's Keep It Catholic.* Washington, DC: NCEA, 2005.

Ravitch, Diane. *The Great School Wars: New York City, 1805–1973.* Baltimore: Johns Hopkins University Press, 1974, 1988.

Recent Vocations to Religious Life: A Report for the National Religious Vocation Conference. Washington, DC: Center for the Applied Research to the Apostolate, 2009.

Schier, Tracy, and Cynthia Russett. *Catholic Women's Colleges in America.* Baltimore: Johns Hopkins University Press, 2002.

Sergiovanni, Thomas. *Leadership for the Schoolhouse.* San Francisco: Jossey-Bass, 1996.

Star, J. "Trouble Ahead for Catholic Schools." *Look* 27, no. 21 (1963): 37–40.

Steinfels, P. "The Church's Sex-Abuse Crisis: What's Old, What's New, What's Needed—and Why." *Commonweal,* April 19, 2002.

Telli, A. "Bertone Praises Vitality of Nashville Dominicans." *Tennessee Register,* August 10, 2007. Accessed November 30, 2011. www.phatmass.com/phorum/topic/71664-cardinal-bertone-praises-nashville-dominicans/.

"Ulysses S. Grant." *Encyclopaedia Britannica's Guide to American Presidents,* 2008. Accessed August 11, 2008. www.britannica.com/presidents/article-9116880.

U.S. Conference of Catholic Bishops. *Renewing Our Commitment to Catholic Elementary and Secondary Schools in the Third Millennium.* Washington, DC: U.S. Conference of Catholic Bishops, 2005.

Walch, Timothy. *Parish School: American Catholic Parochial Education from Colonial Times to the Present.* Washington, DC: NCEA, 2003.

Weber, Francis J. *His Eminence of Los Angeles: James Francis Cardinal McIntyre.* Mission Hills, CA: Saint Francis Historical Society, 1997.

Weber, Msgr. Francis J. *California's Reluctant Prelate: The Life and Times of Right Reverend Thaddeus Amat, C.M. (1811–1878).* Los Angeles: Dawson Book Shop, 1964.

Wheatley, Margaret. *Leadership and the New Science: Discovering Order in a Chaotic World.* San Francisco: Berrett-Koehler, 1992.

Index

151

Sherman, Thomas (SJ), 112–13
Sister Formation Conference, 28
sisters: charisms, 37, 40, 42, 43, 51, 85,
  100, 115, 119, 127, 129; common
  life (and educational philosophy),
  37, 55–56; decline in numbers,
  2, 8, 55, 95, 100; education and
  training, 27–28; garb/habit, 7, 52,
  54; health care, 15, 39, 51, 56;
  legacy, 2, 9, 30, 37, 76, 114, 119,
  128; mentoring, 27–28, 47, 50, 88,
  100, 115, 116, 124; ministries, 40,
  42, 52, 53, 56, 58, 63–64, 69, 73, 76,
  88, 100, 115, 124; novitiate, 25, 27,
  35–37, 39, 41, 50, 60, 71, 95, 100,
  115, 121; placement of, 4, 56–58,
  60–61, 65, 87, 96, 105, 111; renewal
  after Vatican II, 7, 48, 51–62, 74,
  77; research into, 31, 90–91, 115,
  120, 127; schools owned by, 86;
  supervision, 28–30; withdrawal from
  parish schools, 57, 62, 65, 66, 68–79,
  96–98, 112, 114, 119, 121
Sisters of Charity of Leavenworth, 29,
  41–42
Sisters of Charity of the Blessed Virgin
  Mary, 48
Sisters of Mercy, 16, 48, 53, 95
Sisters of St. Francis of the Martyr St.
  George (Alton, IL), 107
Sisters of St. Joseph of Carondelet, 16,
  48, 78
Sisters of St. Joseph of Orange (CA),
  16, 48, 119–20, 129
Sisters of St. Louis: arrival in
  Archdiocese of Los Angeles, 16–26,
  133–39; changes in ministries, 62,
  63–64; establishment in Archdiocese
  of Los Angeles, 26; recruitment,
  16–26
social capital, 91

Spiritual Exercises (Ignatius of Loyola),
  73–74
St. Elizabeth's School (Kansas City,
  MO), 101–2
St. Gertrude's Parish (Chicago), 78,
  135
St. Luke the Evangelist School (St.
  Louis, MO), 81
Star, Jack, 99–101
strategic planning, 66
subsidiarity, 112–13

teaching, 15, 26, 27–33, 91, 94, 95, 98,
  100, 101, 120, 124
Third Plenary Council of Baltimore
  (1884), 3, 14
Traviss, Mary Peter (OP), 27–29, 37,
  44, 72–73, 114, 127
Trinitarian Fathers and Brothers, 69, 73

United States Conference of Catholic
  Bishops (USCCB), 94–95, 127, 142
University Consortium for Catholic
  Education, 110–11
University of Notre Dame, 5, 16, 110,
  127
USCCB. *See* United States Conference
  of Catholic Bishops

Vatican II (1962–1965), 2, 40, 51–54,
  56, 57–58, 60, 71, 77, 78, 79, 93, 98,
  103, 109, 111
Verbeck, Mary Sharon (SCL), 32
vocations to religious life, 18, 22, 47,
  48, 52–53, 54, 55, 70–72, 85, 96,
  107, 119, 129

Walch, Timothy, 9
Weber, Francis J. (monsignor), 16
Wheatley, Margaret, 117
Wolff, Madeleva (CSC), 27–28

~

About the Author

Michael P. Caruso, SJ, is president of St. Ignatius College Prep in Chicago. He has served as the chair of the Department of Educational Leadership at Loyola Marymount University, in Los Angeles, California, and was associate professor of education with an emphasis in Catholic administration. He has written on Catholic school leadership, spirituality in education, and the historic foundations of Catholic education, and has also worked extensively in forming Catholic elementary and high school teachers and administrators in the Diocese of Orange and the Archdiocese of Los Angeles, one of the most diverse Catholic school systems in the United States.

Father Caruso earned his BA from Conception Seminary College in Missouri and his MDiv/STB from St. Mary of the Lake University in Mundelein, Illinois. He was ordained for the Diocese of Kansas City–St. Joseph in Missouri and later entered the Jesuits. Subsequently, he earned his EdD from the University of San Francisco at the Institute of Catholic Educational Leadership.

Father Caruso taught at both DeSmet Jesuit High School in St. Louis, Missouri, and Regis Jesuit High School in Denver, Colorado. He has also worked in college campus ministry at Rockhurst Jesuit University in Kansas City, Missouri.